Discover the Ancient Healing Power of Reiki, Awaken Your Mind, Body, Spirit and Heal Your Life

Chakra Healing, Guided Meditation, Third Eye

G000067565

Claim your FREE Audiobook Now

Autoimmune Healing: Transform Your Health, Reduce Inflammation, Heal the Immune System and Start Living Healthy

Do you have an overall sense of not feeling your best, but it has been going on so long that it's actually normal to you?

If you answered yes to any of these question, you may have an autoimmune disease.

Autoimmune diseases are one of the ten leading causes of death for women in all age groups and they affect nearly 25 million Americans. In fact millions of people worldwide suffer from autoimmunity whether they know it or not.

The good news is that many autoimmune conditions can be reversed through a targeted protocol designed to heal the autoimmune system.

AUTOIMMUNE HEALING

Transform Your Health, Reduce Inflammation, Heal The Immune System and Start Living Healthy

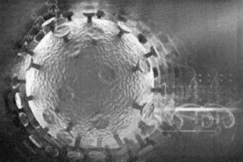

MADISON FULLER

A SPIRITUAL START!

Start your week with gratitude, joy, inspiration, and love.
Healing, motivation, inspiration, challenge and guidance straight to your inbox every week!

FIND OUT MORE

Introduction

This book contains everything you need to know about the ancient healing power of Reiki.

Chapter 1 mainly focuses on the fundamentals of Reiki. It talks about the principles that will enable Reiki practitioners to maintain purity when dealing with others and themselves. It explains the processes that Reiki students need to undergo to eventually become Reiki Masters. It also discusses other important information such as the Chakras, the Reiki levels, the Reiki pillars, the aura cleansing exercises, and the positive impact of Reiki on other healing methods.

Chapter 2 mainly focuses on step-by-step instructions on how to apply Reiki to alleviate or eliminate all the issues that you and others feel mentally, physically, and spiritually. If, for instance, you're still a Reiki student and has not yet completed the student program, there are alternative systems that you can apply to strengthen your healing powers. For those who have completed the program, the step-by-step instructions on how to heal yourself and others are all detailed in this chapter. Also in this chapter, you will be taught the specific techniques to heal relationships, to attract true love, to address financial issues, to get everything that you desire, and, basically, to turn all negativities into positive things.

Chapter 3 mainly focuses on the types of food and drinks that are ideal for your Chakras. Among the subtopics discussed in this chapter are sugar, chocolate, meat, white flour, caffeinated drinks, alcohol, and heavy metals, among others. In this chapter, you will also learn about the different types of diet such as the Raw Food Diet, the Vegetable Diet, and the Vegan Diet. Aside from dietary tips, Chapter 3 also provides tips for exercising.

Chapter 4 mainly focuses on how you can enhance your connection with Reiki itself. Your relationship with the Reiki is significant as this is the basis of how effective your healing powers will be. In this chapter, there are specific sections that will mainly focus on healing old people, babies, and animals.

Chapter 5 offers information on several tools that are significant when you put up your own Reiki healing or wellness center. Among these tools are the Reiki table, the face cradle, and the table sheets.

Chapter 6 mainly talks about the techniques on how you can effectively detect negative energies, how you can prevent them from getting bigger, and how you can eliminate them completely.

By reading this book in its entirety, you will learn how possible it is to completely heal yourself and others through the power of Reiki.

Thanks for downloading this book, I hope you enjoy it!

Chapter 1 - The Reiki Fundamentals

The term "Reiki" originates from two Japanese terms, namely, Rei and Ki which mean Universal Life and Energy, respectively. Contrary to what others think, Reiki is not associated with neither any religious practice nor any religion. It should not be regarded as neither a form of massage nor of a traditional belief. It is an art of healing done by means of the life force energy that is guided by the spirit.

The energy flowing through all human beings and all other living things is the Reiki. Each of us have our own healing energy and if you are able to successfully connect with yours, you may use it to strengthen not only your energy but also the energy of other people – and all other living things, for that matter. If and when your energy is strong, this means that both your mind and body are healthy and in a positive state. A weak or blocked energy means that there is a possibility for you to experience emotional and physical imbalance.

In this chapter, you will learn all the basic things that you need to know about Reiki.

THE REIKI PRINCIPLES

The Reiki principles were developed by the Reiki founder himself, Dr. Mikao Usui. His intention was to help Reiki practitioners to constantly possess purity not only in their words and actions towards others, but also purity in their words and actions towards themselves.

Let us tackle each of these principles.

Principle #1 – Remind yourself not to be angry today

Anger is the most negative emotion there is. In most cases, when you are angry, you feel as if you are in your most powerful state. What you don't realize is that, in reality, it is actually giving you a fallacious sense of power. Anger gives you a wrong belief that it transforms you into a stronger being but, if you notice, you always end up emotionally, physically, and mentally drained. To make matters worse, anger does not resolve things and, therefore, it eventually creates more negative consequences such as more ruined relationships and more illnesses brought about by stress, among others. In other words, anger is one of your greatest enemies, if not the greatest.

Anger blockages may be removed through Reiki. However, Reiki has no power to remove current anger. So, if and when you experience anger and want to get rid of it, you first have to calm yourself down before doing Reiki healing on yourself. It is during this time, among many others, that the "Om" mantra may be used.

The "Om" mantra may be chanted during times when you feel that you are about to burst in anger. Generally, it can help you calm down. But, surprisingly, it also has the ability to transform negative occurrences into positive ones.

The "Om" mantra is also called the "Om" vibration. It originated from both Yoga and Hinduism and is said to have a high spiritual power. But then again, Reiki is not known to promote any religion or any particular religious practice that's why the "Om" mantra may be chanted by anyone freely. In tradition, it is chanted before a yoga session starts and is once again chanted at the end of every session.

This mantra is pronounced as "aum" wherein A is pronounced as "awe," U is pronounced as "oo," and M is pronounced as "mmm." These three letters symbolizes the Shakti, or the divine energy, including its three primary characteristics, namely, liberation, preservation, and creation.

Principle #2 – Remind yourself not to worry today

The inability of man to live in the now is said to be the root cause of all suffering. We worry because of what might transpire in the future. We worry of things that may or may not transpire in the future.

If you are familiar of the law of attraction, it states that whatever we think or create in our minds, we attract them in real life. Therefore, if you worry and think that negative things will happen to you, then chances are, they will really happen to your life. It is basically the same when you think and believe that positive things will happen to your life, you will most likely make these positive things come into reality. In other words, you have the ability to control whether you want your life to be a beautiful one or a disastrous one.

Of course, you might say that it is all easier said than done. We don't really know why it is easier for man to think negatively than to think positively. Nonetheless, there are always methods to avoid yourself from continuously anticipating negative things to happen. One is to learn to list down all your negative thoughts on paper. Pour all your anxieties, fears, and hatred. Then, burn the paper and flush the ashes down the toilet, as if telling the Universe to permanently remove all the worries in you.

At the same time, try starting a journal wherein you can write down all your life goals and visions. It is even advisable to write everything using the present tense, imagining that your goals and visions are all currently transpiring. Also, make it a point to write as positively as possible. You will be amazed at how your life will positively attract wonderful and beautiful things.

Principle #3 – Remind yourself to be grateful today

The most powerful emotion is said to be gratitude because when you are grateful, you are manifesting positivity. When you are grateful, you mostly think of the good and wonderful things only. In the event that negative things enter your mind, you regard them as very minor and are not a big deal at all.

One of the most effective practices on how to be consistently grateful is to create a gratitude journal and list down all the things you are thankful for on a daily basis. You can do this in the morning as soon as you wake up or you can do this in the evening right before you go to bed. That way, you will start and end your day positively.

Another effective approach is to be thankful for something that you actually have not received yet. Being thankful in advance allows you to maintain your positivity. Once you receive it, it only further strengthens your positivity in life. That's why gratitude is regarded as the most powerful emotion as it exhibits nothing but pure positivity.

Principle #4 – Remind yourself to practice honesty and integrity today

Have you heard of that quote by British writer C.S. Lewis wherein he said that, "Integrity is doing the right thing even when no one is watching"? It is actually a great mantra to practice because integrity undoubtedly exudes positivity.

Imagine when you are at work and nobody else knows how to do your tasks except you. Being regarded as an efficient worker, your boss doesn't really check on you often but, instead, he heavily relies on your final output. Knowing that you have already gained the trust of your boss, you then decide to do something dishonest and successfully do away with it without anybody knowing it. You deliver your final output on time and nobody has an inkling about your dishonest action.

What you are not aware of is that your dishonesty creates negativity inside you. You may have successfully done it and that nobody suspects you for your dishonesty but, at the back of your mind, you know that you have done something wrong.

Something is bothering you at the back of your mind, which means that there are negative emotions inside you. Unfortunately, such negative emotions will eventually take a toll on you – this can be related to this thing we call karma. Karma may not happen in relation to the dishonest thing you do at work, but it may manifest in the other aspects of your life – and it will happen all because of the negative emotion residing inside you.

Sometimes, no matter how unwilling you may be to do dishonest things, you are forced to do so especially if you think it will harm no one any way. Sometimes, you do dishonest things because you get rewarded for doing so. It makes you feel as if you won't get rewarded if you do honest things. At times, when you feel this way, remind yourself to nonetheless work and live with integrity. Constantly remind yourself that good deeds will undoubtedly be rewarded – maybe not tomorrow but someday. But, in all honesty, the greatest reward of all when you live with integrity is your opportunity to live with a pure heart and with pure positivity. Indeed, it has a long lasting effect.

Principle #5 – Remind yourself to express kindness today not only to human beings but to all living things

Kindness, just like gratitude and integrity, exhibits positive emotions. When you show your kindness to others, chances are, you will receive kindness as well. Try this when you encounter a rude person who seems to be filled with anger and hatred inside him. Don't retaliate and be rude to him as well. Instead, patiently listen to his rants and react with kindness. Then, notice how he will tame and calm down. Observe how he will somehow feel embarrassed for being rude. Observe how positive emotions are more powerful than the negative ones.

This also exhibits the power of the Golden Rule that states, "Don't do unto others what you don't want others to do unto you." Doesn't it feel good when you know that people regard you as a kind person? If and when you have this reputation, other people will show their kindness to you, too. Indeed, when you exhibit positive emotions, everyone else will respond in a positive manner as well.

This, of course, extends to all living things. Show your kindness, your gentleness, and your love even to animals. They have feelings, too.

THE PROCESSES YOU NEED TO UNDERGO AS A REIKI STUDENT

Your intention to become a Reiki practitioner to heal yourself and others is a lifelong responsibility and, therefore, you must be truly committed to this decision of yours. You must also be informed that there are several processes that you need to undergo as a Reiki student and practitioner. These processes are:

1. Finding the ideal Reiki Master for you. You may inquire about Reiki Masters in spiritual centers, wellness centers, or healing centers. In fact, you may also inquire online by searching for them on the Internet.

2. Attending the Reiki attunement ceremony. This usually lasts for two to three days and may be held one-on-one with your Reiki Master or as a group. Here, you learn the fundamentals of Reiki including its history, the principles, the proper way of healing yourself and others, and allowing yourself to make Reiki form part of your lifestyle.

3. Undergoing the 21 Day Pledge and the Healing Crisis. The Healing Crisis forms part of the 21-Day Pledge in which you will experience a different kind of transformation as well as healing for a period of – yes, you guessed that right – twenty one days. This pledge will actually make or break you as a Reiki practitioner. If and when you are able to survive twenty one days without quitting and your determination and drive to

go on is still the same or even greater, then you will most likely succeed as a Reiki practitioner.

RECEIVING REIKI ATTUNEMENTS

The mere fact that you are reading this book means that you are interested in becoming a Reiki practitioner. However, in order to become one, you must first receive Reiki attunements.

You might ask, are you qualified to receive Reiki attunements? Are you qualified to become a Reiki practitioner? The answer is yes and yes. In fact, there are no special requirements or prerequisites for receiving attunements. You are not even required to extensively know the history of Reiki and everything else there is to know about it – but, of course, if you are truly interested in this Universal Life Energy, you will intentionally and automatically do your best to learn everything about it.

You need not be in excellent health physically, mentally, and emotionally to be eligible to receive Reiki attunements. You can either be young or old too. The only thing that you have to possess is your open-mindedness, your interest, and your willingness to wholeheartedly receive Reiki attunements.

The only person who can provide you Reiki attunements is a Reiki Master.

Attunement Preparations

While there may be no qualifications to become eligible to receive Reiki attunements, there are nonetheless some requirements to ensure that you come prepared when you meet your Reiki Master for your attunements.

First, you have to come in comfortable clothes. Second, you are suggested to wear light-colored clothes. Third, you are advised to drink lots of water before you start the attunement process. You might ask, why do you need such preparation? Well, you have to be in comfortable clothes and you have to be hydrated because the entire attunement process will most likely drain your energy. If you don't feel comfortable and if you get dehydrated, you will surely end up exhausted and over fatigue.

You are also advised to anticipate that you might feel different kinds of emotions during the entire process. This means, feeling both negative and positive emotions. It is anticipated that there are feelings of joy and happiness throughout the process because we all possess positive emotions no matter how negative a person we might be. At the same time, the negative emotions come from unresolved emotions that are residing deep within us. Sometimes, you might feel as if you are an epitome of positivity in front of other people because you radiate nothing but laughter and happiness all the time. What you don't realize is the fact that somehow you deny feeling something negative. You don't entertain negative thoughts but, in reality, you get affected by it. Consciously, you believe that you exude a positive aura. But subconsciously, there is some negative energy residing inside you. This is the reason why during the attunement process, you will be surprised to realize about some unresolved emotions. When this happens, do not worry or be scared. Everyone who goes through the attunement process experiences this. These changes in emotions will absolutely drain you that's why it is best that you come in comfortable clothes and you come dehydrated. Also, most importantly, you have to show up with an open-mind and with utmost interest in Reiki.

Executing the Attunement Process

The attunement process is actually kept a secret by Reiki Masters and all other Reiki practitioners. While everyone knows that all Reiki practitioners have to go through the attunement process, anyone who has received it has not divulged any extensive information about it. Also, those who are interested in receiving Reiki attunements – just like you – will most likely not get any information from any reading material or from the Internet. Surely, they will find information about how they should prepare and what they should expect from the attunement ceremony but no source of information will ever tell them any extensive details. Therefore, you will not know what truly transpires during the Reiki ceremony unless you experience it first-hand.

By the end of the ceremony, however, you will gain knowledge about the various hand techniques, symbols, and positions that are significant in healing both yourself and other people.

Furthermore, due to the fact that Reiki transpires across the physical plane, and perhaps because of the new age technology too, the attunement ceremony may be held face-to-face or remotely between the Reiki Master and the one receiving the Reiki attunements.

Face-to-Face Attunements

The face-to-face attunement process can either be a one-or-one session or a group session. During the session, the Reiki Master will provide you the correct attunements for your level. At the same time, he will demonstrate various hand positions, symbols, and healing strategies ideal for your level.

In most cases, a one-on-one session lasts for a maximum of four hours, in which case, the Reiki Master completes the entire process for a maximum of two days – which translates to two hours per day. In the case of a group session, this normally lasts for six hours, in which case, the Reiki Master completes the entire process for a maximum of three days – which also translates to two hours per day.

Remote Attunements

Since the Universal Life Energy flows through time and space, the attunement process can be done by phone. Reiki practitioners must be thankful for the advent of the Internet as the attunement ceremony can now be done online through FaceTime, Skype, and all other telecommunications application software.

It is possible that aside from video calls, both the Reiki Master and the one receiving the Reiki attunements will also communicate by sending direct messages. The important thing when the attunement process is done remotely is that the communication is real time.

Similar to what the Reiki Master demonstrates during a face-to-face session, he will also provide the correct attunements for you level. At the same time, he will also demonstrate the different hand positions, symbols, and healing methods.

The Three Reiki Attunement Levels

The attunements that you will receive all depend on your own experience with Reiki. If you are a newbie, you belong to Level I in which the Reiki Master will attune you to receive four symbols that will enable you to use Reiki.

If your own Reiki experience is – or has become – more extensive than a newbie, you are then eventually categorized as a Level II Reiki student. The Reiki Master will then attune you to receive three more symbols apart from the four symbols you initially receive as a Level I Reiki student.

The highest attunement level is Level III and is commonly termed as the Reiki Master Level. Aside from the seven symbols you received as a Level I and Level II Reiki student, you now receive a couple of additional symbols. Moreover, your Reiki Master will extensively demonstrate to you how you can eventually and successfully attune others in the future.

Once you complete these three levels of Reiki attunements, you will then become eligible to attune Reiki students.

Experiencing the Healing Crisis

As mentioned earlier, there is a lot of energy – both positive and negative – that will be used up during the Reiki attunement process. After receiving your attunements, you will most probably need to undergo a detoxing process to heal physically and emotionally. This detoxing process will last for approximately thirty days.

This stage is actually called the Healing Crisis in which the Reiki student who received the attunements will experience different symptoms. These symptoms include lightheadedness, lack of appetite, and fever, among others. Do not fear when you experience these symptoms. These are actually indications that you have effectively received the attunements. It should instead give you the assurance that Reiki is healing you so that you will eventually emerge as a strong Reiki practitioner.

This Healing Crisis forms part of the Twenty One Day Pledge as mentioned earlier. For any Reiki student, this stage is considered the most difficult one. However, once you surpass this stage, you will most definitely emerge stronger and become an effective and efficient Reiki practitioner.

Chapter 2 - The Chakras

If you are determined to become a Reiki practitioner, then it is important that you have a knowledge of the Seven Chakras. In general, these chakras are not visible to the naked eye but all Reiki practitioners – and all clairvoyants for that matter – have the ability to see these chakras which can be described as a rotating wheel of energy.

Each individual has seven chakras in him. These chakras are supposed to be swirling simultaneously and have to be aligned with each other. If and when one of the chakras has a blockage, the energy will not flow and will greatly affect all other chakras.

The First Chakra

The Root or Base Chakra

The Base Chakra is apparently considered as the foundation of the whole Chakra system. It is represented by a four-petal deep red lotus and is connected to the fundamental necessities of life, namely, shelter, security, and food. Your Base Chakra gets blocked if you encounter any threat or traumatic experiences related to your three basic life necessities. These experiences can be spine-related health issues, insecurities, or fear of loss, among many others.

The Base Chakra is known to provide a sense of security and stability. Thus, the reason behind its relation to the earth element.

The Second Chakra

The Sacral Chakra

The location of the Sacral Chakra is at the middle of the navel and the genitals, just right at the lower abdomen. It is represented by a six-petal orange lotus and is associated to the element of water. This means that the Sacral Chakra is connected to bodily functions which include sexuality, reproduction, urinary function, and the circulation of bodily fluids. There are different reasons why blockages may occur in the Sacral Chakra, one of which can be due to traumatic sexual experiences.

If your Sacral Chakra is free from any blockage, your sensual awareness or your innovativeness is strongly heightened.

The Third Chakra

The Solar Plexus

The location of the Solar Plexus is right at the abdominal region at the base of the rib cage. It is represented by a ten-petal yellow lotus and is associated to the element of fire. This means that the Solar Plexus concentrates on controlling a person's will and desire to act. It has something to do with vitality and personal power.

This third Chakra, if blocked, may cause such types of illnesses as diabetes, addiction, ulcers, and other ailments related to the stomach. If you have a blocked Chakra, you will most likely lack energy or look terribly exhausted.

The Fourth Chakra

The Heart Chakra

The location of the Heart Chakra is evidently around the location of our physical heart. It is represented by a twelve-petal green lotus and is associated to the element of air. The Heart Chakra is apparently related to the feeling of love and compassion, and connected to the Holy Spirit.

The blockages experienced with the fourth Chakra are often caused by betrayal, relationship problems, and other traumatic emotional experiences. A closed Chakra may result in lack of compassion or indifference. On the other hand, a healthy Heart Chakra exudes unconditional love.

If you have a healthy Heart Chakra, you do not only express unconditional love towards others. In fact, before you show such kind of love towards others, you first exhibit self-love and self-acceptance.

The Fifth Chakra

The Throat Chakra

The location of the Throat Chakra is evidently at the base of the throat. It is represented by a sixteen-petal bright blue lotus and is associated to the element of ether. The Throat Chakra has something to do with our creative expression or our ability to communicate. This means that this fifth Chakra focuses on both our speaking and listening abilities.

If your Throat Chakra has a blockage, you will have a difficult time expressing your feelings and your thoughts. If your Throat Chakra is healthy, you will find yourself efficiently communicating with others.

The Sixth Chakra

The Third Eye

The location of the Third Eye is between our eyebrows. It is represented by a two-petal indigo lotus and is associated to psychic powers. An individual with an awakened third eye has the capability to envision things beyond his five basic senses.

This sixth Chakra is associated to the pineal gland. If your Third Eye has any blockage, you are most likely scared of the mere thought of ghosts. You also tend to exaggeratedly worry about your future. Moreover, you find it difficult to see the truth in any given situation and you seem to have a difficult time processing any kind of information. However, all these can be addressed if you practice Reiki on a regular basis.

The Seventh Chakra

The Crown Chakra

The location of the Crown Chakra is above the head. It is represented by a thousand-petal violet lotus and is associated to the Higher Consciousness, evidently having a relation to the Universe in general.

If your seventh Chakra does not have any blockage, you will most likely experience ultimate enlightenment. Otherwise, you might feel various kinds of negative emotions such as loneliness, feeling disconnected, and chronically depressed, among others.

THE TWO REIKI LEVELS
Reiki Level 1

This level highlights self-healing and every Reiki practitioner has to go through this level. Once you undergo Level 1, you will observe how relaxing self-healing is. It will give you an ultimate feeling of rejuvenation. In order to make this a truly effective session, you have to have full concentration and you have to practice this every single day for a period of twenty one days. Otherwise, you will not realize its true impact on yourself. Besides, not completing the 21-day period means that you will not complete your Level 1 session.

There are a few important reminders prior to the start of your Reiki session. First, you have to ensure that you are not wearing any watch or any other kind of jewelry or clothing accessory for that matter. This is important as any type of metal might hinder the way energy is transmitted from the Reiki Master to you.

Second, if you are currently taking any medication, you are advised to still take it religiously. Just because you know that Reiki healing can help you feel better, it doesn't necessarily mean that you should stop the medications prescribed to you by your doctor. Reiki healing is expected to make you feel better. In fact, it can even quicken your recovery. However, whatever your physician has advised you, you are still advised to follow their medical advice.

Third, fix your schedule and allot an ample time for your Reiki session. Make sure to have a fixed schedule and strictly follow it. In most cases, Reiki practitioners conduct sessions before they go to bed as this helps them get a good night's sleep.

Fourth, consider the 21-day period your detoxification period. The detox period does not only focus on healing you physically but it also effectively heals you mentally and emotionally, thus, rejuvenating your entire energy level. Again, be mindful that unwanted memories and emotions might resurface as it is all part of self-healing. You may find this difficult to handle but, no matter how hard it may be, just continue the session until you complete the entire Level 1 session. Always remind yourself not to quit. After all, your ultimate goal is to become a full-fledged Reiki practitioner.

Fifth, consistently drink enough water to prevent yourself from getting dehydrated. As earlier mentioned, the session will most likely drain you mentally, emotionally, and physically. It is best that you are always hydrated. Besides, you may also consider this as your water therapy.

Sixth, during the entire Level 1 session, refrain from going to crowded places or from attending parties. You are not really prohibited from doing so but unavoidable circumstances might lead you to negative situations. Additional negative experiences will aggravate your self-healing process. Your detoxification is a critical period and you might end up draining all your energy if you force yourself to attend parties and join a crowd.

Seventh, avoid doing negative things. Remind yourself to always practice kindness and to always do good deeds. This way, you will prevent yourself from encountering additional negative experiences and the self-healing process will not be that difficult for you.

Eighth, Reiki healing may be practiced anytime. This means that once you know how to do self-healing, you have the authority to practice it anytime and anywhere you may be. In fact, it is advisable that once you learn the process, you have to practice it outright and on a regular basis until you become an expert on it.

Ninth, you have to be mindful of every part of your body. Be thankful for each and every part of you. Practice self-love. Be gentle to yourself. Treat yourself the way you want to be treated by others.

Lastly, always think and do things in a positive manner. Even as you undergo the Level 1 session in which your energy will be drained, remind yourself that the difficulty you are experiencing will soon be over. Remind yourself that you will soon be rewarded as soon as you surpass the complex period of detoxification.

Executing the Level 1 Session

The Level 1 Reiki session starts with an invocation and followed by reciting the Reiki principles that we discussed earlier. The invocation is expected to augment your vibrational frequency and it is expected to align you with the maximum healing energy level.

Your Reiki Master will recite to you the words you both need to utter during the invocation. These words vary and it all depends on the Reiki Master. However, no matter how different the words used, it all has the same meaning, and it goes something like this:

"Right this very moment, I invoke in my heart the light of the Universe in its purest form;

I am blessed to have been considered as a perfect channel for the Universe's divine love;

The light of God is illuminating in every part of me;

Into me and through me, the power of God flows."

Again, the words used by Reiki Masters may be different. But once you absorb what your Reiki Master utters, you will realize that the words used in the invocation have one and the same meaning.

How to Treat Others Using Reiki Healing Level 1

While Reiki Healing Level 1 initially focuses on self-healing, you will also be capable of treating others as soon as you have completed your initiation. The hand positions used for self-healing are basically the same as those used for healing others. It's just that, apparently, the hands are placed on another person.

To start treating others, you have to instruct your patient to lie down comfortably and continuously take deep breaths until they feel relaxed. This way, it will be easier for the patient to receive healing and it will be easier for you to heal him.

However, prior to the start of the healing process, you must execute Kenyoku, or what is commonly termed as dry bathing. This will be taught to you by your Reiki Master. Kenyoku will allow you to disconnect yourself from the negative energies that surround you, including the negative energies harboring inside your patient. Moreover, Kenyoku will not only shield you from those negative energies, but it will also remove the negative energies inside you. This means that as you are healing a patient, you are healing yourself as well.

Reiki Level 2

More than anything else, the priority of Reiki Healing Level 1 is self-healing. This is so because the self-healing session prepares you for the Level 2 session. Before you begin with this second level, you are expected to have mastered the first level. After all, you have undergone it for a minimum of 21 consecutive days – after which, you are expected to continue practicing it on a daily basis. If you are practicing Level 1 on a regular basis, then you will most likely be able to handle the second level well.

The completion of Reiki Healing Level 1 session also strengthens your faith and belief in the power of Reiki

Healing. Therefore, if you have mastered this, practicing and mastering the second level will surely be no mean feat for you.

Learning Distance Healing

In Reiki Healing Level 2, you will learn distance healing. In this type of healing, your ability to send healing energy to your patient will not be limited by time and space. In general, this may seem unreal. However, this phenomenon is starting to be acknowledged by science as there are now existing studies to support it. There are research findings indicating that we are all one and living in an interconnected Universe.

We all have our knowledge of our own truth. Through Reiki Healing Level 2, you will realize that there is a whole lot more beyond our limited knowledge of the truth. You will come to a realization of what infinite and eternal truly mean. During your first experience of conducting distance healing, you will most likely feel skepticism about its effectiveness. Your patient is expected to feel the same way. If and when this happens, just continue conducting the healing process as it will nonetheless be effective. As you go on, you and your patient will feel its effectiveness. This will then lead both of you to strengthen your faith in the entire process and, before you realize it, the healing process will start to become more and more profound.

When you complete your initiation process, you will undergo once again an energy detoxification process that you have to endure for 21 consecutive days – again, you need to undergo the 21-day period. There is likelihood that more negative memories and emotions will resurface, which did not resurface as you undergo the first level. Do not fear if and when you encounter this. Remind yourself that it will all be for the better. You will feel rejuvenated sooner or later.

So, in this level, you will be equipped to heal yourself, heal others face-to-face, and heal others even from a distance. Your ability to conduct distance healing encompasses not only physical healing but also emotional and mental healing. You will encounter patients with complex physical, mental, and emotional issues but even through distance healing, you will be able to help them effectively. Indeed, Reiki Healing knows no boundaries.

In Reiki Healing Level 2, you are still advised to conduct self-healing using the same hand positions and healing techniques you learned in Reiki Healing Level 1. You might ask if there is any difference between Level 1 and Level 2 healing. The answer is yes because self-healing is faster in the second level.

Before you start healing yourself and others, make sure to strictly undergo initiation from your Reiki Master. You will definitely not go wrong by doing so.

THE REIKI PILLARS

The Reiki Healing is composed of three pillars which are all connected to the five Reiki Principles we discussed earlier. During Dr. Usui's retreat where he learned about the Reiki symbols, these pillars also appeared before him. These Reiki pillars are Gassho, Reiji-Ho, and Chiryo. Let's discuss each one of them in this section.

Gassho

This pillar is a ritual gesture that signifies gratitude and respect. It is done by placing both your hands in a prayer position. Gassho is an ideal practice for being mindful as the acts of gratitude and respect successfully bring you into the present. These acts also result in inner peace and sense of balance. It is also considered as the representation of the Universal consciousness.

According to Dr. Usui, the Gassho meditation must be practiced twice a day – a maximum of twenty minutes in the morning and another twenty minutes in the evening. All Reiki students are advised to practice the Gassho meditation before they begin their Reiki session.

The step-by-step instructions for executing the Gassho meditation are as follow:

1. You must find a comfortable sitting position and make sure that you are sitting up straight.

2. Place your hands in front of your chest in a Gassho position.

3. Gently close your eyes and take deep breaths.

4. Be mindful of how your hands are positioned, from the way the bottom part of your palms touch up to how the tip of your middle fingers meet.

5. In general, be mindful of what you are doing – the way your hands are placed together, the way you sit, the position of your feet, and so on.

6. In the event that other thoughts enter your mind, entertain those thoughts for a few seconds before you let them go. If you avoid acknowledging those thoughts, they will keep on coming back and all the more that it will distract your Gassho meditation. After entertaining those thoughts, revert back to meditation.

7. After 20 minutes of meditation, rub both of your palms together before you gently cover your eyes with them. Then, as you place your hands on your lap, gently open your eyes and absorb the positive feeling brought about by the Gassho meditation.

Reiji-Ho

The Reiji-Ho is another pillar that forms part of the series of rituals that you should practice before you conduct a Reiki session. The following are the step-by-step instructions to perform the Reiji-Ho ritual:

1. Gently close your eyes as you place your hands in front of your chest in a Gassho position.

2. Make a heartfelt declaration of your willingness to connect yourself with the Reiki Healing energy. Repeat your declaration three times. If you have already completed your Reiki Healing Level 2 initiation, then feel free to apply the Reiki symbols.

3. Be mindful of how the Reiki Healing energy will enter your body through the Crown Chakra. It will then flow into your heart as well as into the palms of your hand.

4. Say a prayer for your Reiki patient, emphasizing on his healing and good health. Also, mention your intention to become his source of healing energy.

5. As you continue to be in the Gassho position, continue saying your prayer and allow it to reach your third eye. Request the Reiki energy to guide you as you conduct healing to your patient.

6. Start giving healing by placing your hands above your patient. Allow your intuition to guide your hands to hover over the right areas. You will also notice that your intuition will guide you as to when you should move your hands from one region to another. Simply go with the flow. At the same time, be mindful of what you are doing. Maintain the purity of your intention to heal. Never judge or think negatively of your patient.

7. As soon as you're done with the healing session, let the palms of your hands touch your lap. Then, once again, gently place your hands in the Gassho position.

8. During your first time to conduct a healing session on a patient, you might find yourself getting affected with both the positive and negative energies brought about by the emotions residing inside him. Practice to detach yourself from your patient's emotions. There will come a time when you will have to heal more than one patient

in one day. If you always allow yourself to get affected, you will most likely get exhausted even before the day ends.

Chiryo

Chiryo is the last ritual that completes the three Reiki pillars. It's a Japanese term that literally means "treatment" in English. The following are the step-by-step instructions for executing a Chiryo ritual:

1. Just like the first two pillars that we have discussed, your hands must initially be in the Gassho position.

2. Gently place your dominant hand above the head of the patient as you start to pray for his healing. Continue to pray until you feel the momentum arising, which can only be achieved when you surrender all your doubts and your thoughts in general.

3. Once you feel the momentum and the inspiration to start healing, you will find your dominant hand automatically hovering from above the patient's head to other parts of the body. You might also be awed by your experience as you find your hand moving to areas where your patient needs healing the most.

LEARNING EXERCISES FOR AURA CLEANSING

Every individual, or any living thing for that matter, has an aura. It is a one-of-a-kind magnetic field that surrounds a person's physical body and its size is based on the level of his spiritual growth. For instance, a person filled with negativity inside him may only have an aura that's a few inches thick, while a person filled with positivity residing inside him may have a thick or wide aura that can extend up to a few kilometers.

Everything you think of has an impact on your aura. Your aura changes constantly, depending on what your thoughts are. If you are caught up in a negative situation and you are deeply affected by it, chances are that the aura surrounding your body will appear thin. Whereas, if you have been receiving good news for the last few days, this will definitely brighten your aura in which its brightness may probably extend for even a kilometer or so. However, the brightness of your aura fluctuates and it all depends on what your thoughts are and how badly you are affected by those thoughts. In most cases, if not all, clairvoyants are the only ones who get to notice how quick – or how slow – your auras change from positive to negative, and vice versa.

Everybody's familiar of what the term "personal hygiene" means but not everyone knows that there's also this thing called "spiritual hygiene." Everybody has to have spiritual hygiene. This means that you have to keep your aura clean all the time to protect it from damage or further damage caused by your negative emotions. If and when you are spiritually hygienic, you will consistently display joy and happiness in public. Your positivity will then be contagious and you will successfully encourage other people to also be happy, positive, and energetic at all times. Furthermore, your spiritual hygiene will allow you to attract more and more positive things in life.

There's this so-called Aura Cleansing Exercise and it's important that you practice this on a daily basis even before you begin conducting your daily Reiki healing or self-healing session. In fact, before you start any kind of meditation session, you are recommended to first do the Aura Cleansing Exercise before doing anything else. This exercise is best done first thing in the morning as soon as you wake up and then another set in the evening before you start any healing session in the evening.

Below are the step-by-step instructions for doing the Aura Cleansing Exercise:

- Find a comfortable sitting position. You can either sit on a chair or do the Indian-style sitting position on the floor. While doing so, make sure that you're keeping your back straight.

- Start taking slow and deep breaths to make you feel relaxed and comfortable. Consistently apply this breathing exercise until the end of your Aura Cleansing Exercise.

- You have the option to open or close your eyes as you do the exercise. However, it is preferred that you have your eyes closed to prevent yourself from getting distracted. So, for the sake of this discussion, let's agree on keeping your eyes closed.

- As you gently close both of your eyes, create a mental image of a bright light bulb hanging right above your head and shining down on you. Imagine the light shining around your entire body. Imagine that to be your aura.

- Now, as you hold that image in your mind, add an image of an enormous golden comb with thick bristles. Imagine that there's an invisible hand holding the comb and combing your aura as if it were a long, thick hair.

  In reality, when you comb your hair, you always notice some hair strands falling off and go straight on the floor. This is particularly noticeable among women with long hair. Apply this in the mental images that you have created. Visualize strands falling off your aura as the comb moves from top to bottom. However, instead of hair strands, the strands that fall off are the negative thoughts and emotions residing inside you. Allow all "negative strands" to fall down and replace them with positive thoughts and emotions.

- Continuously allow the invisible hand to comb your aura until you one hundred percent feel that you have been freed from all negative thoughts and emotions.

- As soon as you're done, continue to close your eyes and create a mental image of yourself enclosed in a golden pyramid. Imagine that you are inside that pyramid and it helps you preserve your positivity. The pyramid is filled with positive energies and these energies are all surrounding you. The pyramid serves as your shield to prevent negative energies from getting near you.

  The pyramid will cause the negative energies to bounce back to the Universe and transform to positive energies before it goes back to the sender. This means that you are not simply shielding yourself from negativity, but you are also sharing your blessing to others by sending positive energies their way. Besides, when you share your blessings, you will surely receive more blessings in life.

- Once you feel you are ready to end your Aura Cleansing Exercise, you may start to gently open your eyes. You are now ready to perform Reiki healing sessions for the entire day.

- Again, always remind yourself to do this exercise before starting any Reiki healing session.

ENHANCING THE LIFE FORCE ENERGY

For sure you have noticed how some women don't seem to be beautiful in a conventional way but you don't understand why people in general find them highly attractive just by merely looking at them. This goes out to men as well. Also, people in general describe them as people with the X-factor. Well, for Reiki practitioners, they are described as people with a positive life force energy.

On the contrary, there are also people whom we feel reluctant to approach. For instance, you are inside a bank and you need to talk to a customer service representative. You then look around and saw a woman who forms part of the Customer Service Department. The woman is beautiful. From afar, you can hear her talking on the phone and you notice that she indeed has a pleasant voice. But you feel reluctant to approach her. You also notice that nobody seems to be talking to her and her co-workers don't seem to be interested in making small talks with her. Why? Because deep inside her is a negative life force energy. People don't enjoy talking to her, hanging out with her, or being in her presence. No matter how beautiful a woman may be, people will dislike her if she exudes negativity.

There are times when a person with a negative life force energy outwardly exhibits a bad behavior. For instance, the person never fails to criticize all his co-workers, he is always annoyed, and he is always upset. On the contrary, a person with a negative life force energy can be someone who already exudes negativity just by merely looking at him. In general, people don't want to approach them no matter how handsome or beautiful they may be.

Having said that, this only goes to show how energy communicates with each and every individual.

All individuals have a life force energy. As a matter of fact, all living things do have. A big life force energy means that you are happy and healthy. Of course, the bigger it is, the happier and healthier you are.

Below are several tips on how you can enhance and / or constantly maintain a positive life force energy:

- Live with integrity. Always promote honesty because it promotes confidence and positivity. On the contrary, doing dishonest things results in fear which creates negative emotions. Apparently, if you continuously live in dishonesty, you will exhaust all your positive life force energy.

- When you talk to yourself or to others, practice to always speak from the heart. That way, you are speaking with pure intentions because you're saying what you're also feeling inside. This means that your words and your feelings are both in sync with each other. Otherwise, if you force yourself to say things that don't come from the heart, you will deplete your positive life force energy.

- Prevent yourself from getting angry easily. In fact, you have to prevent yourself from getting angry at all times. This may not be an easy task but you will surely consider this as a big achievement once you learn to control yourself. If and when you find yourself caught up in a situation that you know will eventually lead to your anger, refrain yourself from getting angry and, instead, express positivity by blessing that person or the situation. In other words, if and when you practice unconditional love in general, you will succeed in preventing yourself from feeling angry.

  You might ask if there's such a person who doesn't get angry. Well, the answer is yes. They have practiced and mastered how to be understanding at all times – to take into consideration every aspect of a situation and they always give the benefit of the doubt. If these people were able to do this successfully, it only means that you can do it too.

- Practice being loving and compassionate at all times. This is related to the previous tip mentioned because, here, you also have to practice and master unconditional love.

  Unconditional love is considered to be the most profound way of enhancing every individual's positive life force energy. Once you master exhibiting unconditional love, you will be amazed with how each aspect of your life becomes positive – and how your life will generally become happier and healthier.

- Bless every individual that you meet on a daily basis. Every time someone approaches you, warmly welcome that person and, in your mind and heart, silently wish him to have a happy life at all times. As he approaches, show that you are interested in what he's about to tell you and show him that you are interested in helping him.

  This behavior basically goes back to the most profound way of enhancing your positive life force energy which is to express unconditional love. Sharing your blessings forms part of unconditional love and when you share your blessings, expect that you will also be blessed a hundred times more.

- If you have vices, it's about time that you get rid of all of them. If you drink alcoholic beverages, you are highly encouraged to stop. If you smoke, you are encouraged to stop just as much. If you are male and you womanize, you are of course encouraged to stop womanizing too – and this apparently goes out to their female counterparts. In other words, let go of all the negative things that you constantly do. Let go of your bad habits and your negative lifestyle. Replace them with good habits and a positive lifestyle. The succeeding tips will tell you how to create a positive lifestyle.

- Aside from your regular meditation sessions through Reiki, it is best that you also exercise. If your conception of exercising is to make you physically attractive, well, sorry to burst your bubble but that is a secondary thing only. If you're currently not into working out or exercising, try asking questions to those who visit the gym on a regular basis. You will learn that looking good as far as their physical appearance is concerned is not their number one priority – in fact, it's just a bonus to them that they turn out to be physically good looking.

More than anything else, exercising makes them stronger not only physically but also mentally and even emotionally. Amazingly, exercising will make you feel better inside and out, thus, clearing your mind, heart, and body from all the negativities. That's why consistently working out will also allow you to consistently live positively.

- Practice and master eating a healthy diet by always adding a generous amount of vegetables in your every meal. Always buy organic vegetables and eat as much as raw vegetables as you can. If not, slightly cook or steam them to maintain their freshness.

  For those who are not vegetable lovers, this might quite be a difficult thing to do. If you are one of them, believe that it's not impossible to do and trust that you can do it. Many Reiki practitioners had never eaten vegetables before until they have started to engage themselves in the Reiki practice. Like you, they never thought that they would eventually learn to eat vegetables.

- Aside from vegetables, learn to eat organic fruits too. In general, majority of the people eat fruits but, the sad part is, majority of the people don't eat fruits every day. Though some eat fruits daily, fruits only form part of their dessert.

  This time, you are encouraged to eat fruits and make it part of each of your main meal. For instance, instead of eating burger and fries for lunch, you might as well replace them with fruits and vegetables.

- Of course, once you learn to make organic fruits and vegetables part of your daily meal, you should also learn to drink beverages that are made out of fresh fruits and / or vegetables.

- Oblige yourself to strictly follow all these tips for twenty one consecutive days and you will be surprised at how you have adjusted well to doing all of these things. Amazingly, you will find yourself normally and naturally practicing all these things and that there's no need to force yourself anymore. If and when this happens, it only means that you have replaced your old unhealthy lifestyle with a new and healthy one. Now, try it!

THE IMPACT OF REIKI ON OTHER HEALING METHODS

If a person is suffering from an illness or has experienced deep trauma, he will most likely seek professional medical help. Similarly, if an animal experiences deep trauma or is suffering from an illness, its owner or master will most likely seek the help of a veterinarian. Rarely – or hardly – would it ever occur that they would first consider to go and see a Reiki healer.

This is fine. After all, they're known to be professionals. Besides, those who seek healing from Reiki Masters are not instructed to stop seeking professional and medical help. Reiki is known to be a supplement that can effectively be combined with alternative medicine, psychological, and medical treatment to achieve amazing results. In fact, there are a number of medical professionals who have been applying Reiki in their practice.

Before you conduct Reiki healing on your patient, make sure that it is clear to him that he still has to take the medications prescribed to him by his doctors. Clarify to him the purpose of Reiki and how it can help him feel better.

Chapter 3 Using Reiki as a Healing and Personal Growth System

ALTERNATIVE SYSTEMS FOR REIKI HEALING

There are over a thousand types of Reiki Healing techniques and they are all based on several divisions of Reiki Healing treatments. Healing styles may be different but they are all inspired by the traditional Usui Reiki symbols and methods.

Unfortunately, not all Reiki Healing techniques have been well documented. Those that have been documented are what are being regularly practiced by Reiki practitioners up until today. Let's discuss some of these techniques in this section:

1. **Sacred Flame or Violet Flame**

   This Reiki Healing technique has a fair amount of similarity to the traditional technique of Usui Reiki. The main differences, however, lie on the capability of the Reiki Master to create his own symbols and that the Reiki practitioner is required to receive seven additional attunements. Other than that, all the other Reiki styles applied in this technique are the same as that applied in the traditional method.

2. **Raku Kei**

   The Raku Kei technique features self-healing approaches and symbols that were not taught by Dr. Usui himself. Instead, they were retrieved from Dr. Usui's personal archives. Dr. Usui did not teach these approaches and symbols, but Reiki practitioners believed that they had been used as significant supplements to the tradition method that we know of today.

3. **Karmic**

The Karmic healing system features a combination of distance healing – learned in Reiki Healing Level II as previously discussed – and karma based on Hindu principals. This technique apparently tends to heal and, at the same time, evaluate the person's past experiences as well as his current behavior to make sure that he learns his lessons, heals, and becomes motivated to do positive things to attract positive karma at all times.

4. Celtic

In the Celtic technique, Usui Reiki methods and symbols are both applied. However, they are combined with early Celtic symbols and healing methods. Reiki practitioners who have tried the Celtic technique describe this to be an amazingly soothing and grounding method. In most cases, this technique is practiced in such environments as the forest, woodland, backwoods, and the like.

5. Chios Energy Healing

The Chios Energy Healing technique is a combination of the aura healing methods and the traditional Kundalini Chakra healing methods. When doing the traditional Kundalini Reiki healing method, the Reiki practitioner must first strictly perform yoga prior to the healing session. On the contrary, the Reiki practitioner doesn't have to perform yoga anymore prior to performing the Chios Energy Healing technique. Some practitioners prefer this healing technique because of the fact that it can heal auras too.

6. Blue Star Celestial

The Blue Star Celestial healing system originated from the energetic healing methods used by the early Egyptians. Those ancient methods were believed to be established based on the star constellations positioned above the pyramids. Reiki practitioners who apply this healing system is expected to be insightful of the Egyptians' cosmic-related energy healing approaches.

7. Osho Neo

This particular healing technique was developed by spiritual master Osho Rajneesh. An ardent practitioner of Kundalini Reiki, Master Rajneesh wanted to develop a new Reiki approach that would feature the traditional symbols taught by Dr. Usui combined with Kundalini Yoga methods and Chakra healing methods. The outcome, apparently, is what we now call the Osho Neo method.

8. Kundalini

This healing technique may only be done by performing Kundalini Yoga. This is so because the Reiki practitioner has to open the seven chakras in order to access his internal energy system. This healing technique can never be effective without doing Kundalini Yoga.

9. Rainbow

This healing technique was developed by Reiki Master Walter Lubek. Master Lubek was a student of Madame Hawayo Takata who was one of the first few notable Reiki Masters. This system digs into both the higher-conscious and the subconscious minds to convert illnesses and pains into radiating health and balance. Pretty much like the other healing techniques, the Rainbow technique ensures that healing is done at spiritual, emotional, mental, and physical levels.

10. Karuna

The Karuna healing technique was created by Usui Reiki Master William Lee Rand. Master Rand was also the International Center for Reiki Training founder.

Karuna is a Sanskrit term that means compassion. This technique is heavily based on the traditional system of Usui Reiki and, therefore, works in a similar way. The main difference, however, lies in the fact that the Karuna technique features eight symbols created by Master Rand himself. These symbols are expected to improve the way the Reiki practitioner and his student express compassion.

Practicing Alternative Reiki Healing Systems

If you plan to practice any of the alternative Reiki healing techniques we have discussed, make sure that you are intensively guided by your Reiki Master. This is so because of the special attunements that need to be done aside from the Reiki attunements you initially receive from your Reiki Master.

Aside from seeking guidance from your Reiki Master, you are advised to conduct your own research as well. If you are highly interested in learning about these techniques, then you should definitely find time in gaining wide knowledge about each one of these healing systems. You can meet up with other Reiki practitioners who are also interested in practicing alternative healing systems or you can find a mentor – oftentimes, your Reiki Master is your mentor – who can guide you all the way. Another option is to conduct research all by yourself. In this day and age, it is not difficult to find information about these things as everything is already available on the Internet. One of the recommended strategies when looking for online information is to join social media groups composed of Reiki Masters and practitioners. They surely will all be willing to help you. At the same time, you can also share your own insights with them.

REIKI HEALING TECHNIQUES FOR YOURSELF

Level 1

Once you are capable of conducting self-healing techniques, you are advised to practice self-healing on a daily basis. This will not only allow you to master the techniques but it will also become truly beneficial for your spiritual, emotional, mental, and physical well-being. It will allow you to strengthen your intuition, maintain or improve your sense of balance and calmness, avoid feeling stressed, and feel more at peace. Moreover, it allows you to explore the techniques every day, giving you the opportunity to explore and experiment different approaches. This will not only improve you as a Reiki practitioner but also to hone your skills as a future Reiki Master.

Where to Conduct Self-Healing Sessions?

There are no rules when it comes to the location where you want to conduct your self-healing sessions. You can do it inside your bedroom or any other private area of your choice, or you can do it in a park or any other public location. The important thing is that you can concentrate and effectively perform your self-healing sessions.

Ideally, of course, the location has to be quiet to help you successfully achieve a meditative state. Since you are a beginner, you may want to start conducting self-healing sessions in a quiet setting. Eventually, you can explore public locations like the park. Your concentration will surely be challenged as there will most likely be kids playing and screaming or there will be dogs barking, among other things. However, once you master conducting self-healing sessions in public places, you can then conduct it anywhere you may be.

How Often and How Long Should a Self-Healing Session Be Done?

Traditionally, a self-healing session should be practiced once a day for at least thirty minutes. However, it's all up to you if you want to exceed thirty minutes and if you want to conduct it more than once a day. The important thing is that you don't let a day pass without practicing the self-healing techniques and you don't practice it for less than thirty minutes.

Most Reiki practitioners conduct sessions twice a day. They prefer doing a session first thing in the morning for an hour and then another one-hour session in the evening before they go to bed. That way, they will start and end the day feeling good and at peace.

Why are Daily Self-Healing Sessions Beneficial?

If you have tried exercising or if you have tried attending a yoga session, you definitely know how good the feeling is after every session. The effect is pretty much the same when you strictly conduct self-healing sessions on a daily basis – but the effect is more profound physically, spiritually, mentally, and emotionally. Self-healing will truly help you get rid of negative things such as sprains, muscle tensions, bloating, nervousness, depression, anxiety, stress, and other kinds of pain. Self-healing repairs, balances, and cleanses body organs, tissues, and cells.

What are the Different Hand Positions and Methods for Self-Healing?

The hand positions and methods for self-healing are all based on the traditional techniques for Usui Reiki healing. As time went by, some of these hand positions and methods have eventually been modified, depending on how they are personally done by Reiki practitioners. As previously mentioned in this book, Reiki practitioners are free to explore and conduct some experiments on these hand positions and methods so that they can identify the strategies that work best for them. In this section, however, we will discuss the hand positions and strategies that are applied in general.

First Position: Place Your Palms Over Your Eyes

Cover your eyes with your hands. Your hands should be positioned horizontally over your eyes, in such a way that the tip of your middle fingers touch each other. This position focuses on the third eye chakra and can help heal health issues related to different body parts and organs which include the pineal gland, the pituitary gland, the brain, the sinuses, and the eyes. There are several illnesses that can be cured using this first position which include flus, colds, allergies, fevers, stress, anxiety, migraines, headaches, eye stress, and eye strain, among others.

Second Position: Place Each Palm on Each Side of Your Neck

Place your left palm on the left side of your neck and your right palm on the right side of your neck, just below your ears. This position focuses on the throat chakra and can help heal health issues related to different body parts and organs near the neck which include the thyroid, vocal chords, lymph nodes, pulmonary arteries, esophagus, and the lungs. The ailments that this position can cure include laryngitis, asthma, heart and artery issues, thyroid and lymphatic diseases, among others. This position also addresses stage fright or the fear of speaking in public. Moreover, this position helps in ensuring clarity of communication.

Third Position: Place Your Palms on Your Breastbone

Place the palms of your hands on your breastbone underneath your collarbone. Position your hands horizontally, in such a way that the tip of your middle fingers are touching. This position focuses on the heart chakra and can help heal health issues related to different organs and parts of the body which include the breasts, the thymus gland, the heart, and the upper lungs. Among the illnesses that this position can help cure are breast cancer, heart problems, pneumonia, asthma, and chronic stress or anxiety. This third position can also help heal matters related to passion, self-love, love for others, and relationships.

Fourth Position: Place Your Palms on Your Chest

Place the palms of your hands on your chest, just above your stomach and below your collarbone. Position your hands horizontally in such a way that the tip of your middle fingers are touching. This means that from the third position, you simply slide your hands downwards to achieve the fourth position.

Apparently, the third and fourth positions are connected to each other. The fourth position also brings healing to all pains and illnesses mentioned earlier in the third position.

Fifth Position: Place Your Palms on Your Stomach Area

Place the palms of your hands on the stomach area. Again, your hands should be positioned horizontally in such a way that the tip of your middle fingers are touching. This position focuses on the Solar Plexus Chakra and can help heal health issues related to different organs and parts of the body which include the kidneys, the liver, the gallbladder, the pancreas, and the stomach, among others.

The Solar Plexus Chakra is related to creativity. That's why if you lack inspiration at anything, be it about work or life in general, you must greatly focus on this position.

Sixth Position: Place Your Palms Between Your Groin and Your Stomach

Place the palms of your hands below your stomach but above your groin. Again, your hands should be positioned horizontally in such a way that the tip of your middle fingers are touching. This position can help heal health issues related to different organs and parts of the body which include the colon, and both the large and small intestines. It is connected to the fifth position that's why the sixth position further strengthens healing related to the digestive tract such as bowel problems.

Seventh Position: Place the Palms of Your Hands on Your Groin Area

Place both of your hands, palms facing down, on your groin area. Still connected to the fifth and sixth positions, this seventh position allows additional healing related to the digestive tract and the urinary tract systems. It also helps heal health issues related to your hormones and the reproductive system. This position focuses on the Root Chakra and can help heal matters connected to such aspects as financial, safety, and security.

Step-By-Step Instructions for Self-Healing Meditation (30-45 Minutes)

1. Find a comfortable position before you start your self-healing meditation. You have the option to sit down or lie down. In fact, you may even stand if you want to, but this might not be a comfortable position for you especially if your session lasts for 45 minutes. In most cases, Reiki practitioners conduct self-healing meditation while sitting down. You have the option to sit on a chair or you may sit Indian-style on the floor.

   While lying down may be more comfortable than sitting down, doing the former may cause you to fall asleep. You might end up not completing your meditation session.

   For the sake of our discussion, let's agree on doing the Indian-style sit. After all, it is the most ideal and common position among Reiki practitioners.

2. Gently close your eyes and start to take slow and deep breaths. Do this repeatedly until you feel your neck and shoulders softened. Continue doing so until you notice each part of your body relax – from your head to your arms and hands, to your upper body, then down to your hips, your thighs, your knees, your lower legs, your ankles, your feet, and toes. Continue taking slow and deep breaths until you achieve the state of peace and calmness.

3. As you breathe in and out, clasp your hands together and place them on your chest where you can directly feel your heartbeat. In your most comfortable state, allow Reiki healing to enter your mind and body through the palms of your hands. Allow Reiki to free both your physical and spiritual bodies from any negative force. Once you achieve the state of peace and calmness, it means that you are prepared to start your self-healing session.

4. Start the self-healing session by scanning your aura. Hover your hands from one body part to another, starting from your Crown chakra and down to the other body parts until you reach your toes. Feel the burning sensation you feel in the palms of your hands as you move them. If you detect or feel any blockage, take your time to hover your palms on that particular body part until you feel relieved and better. Be mindful and follow your intuition. You will be amazed that your hands don't seem to want to hover to another body part yet. They seem to want to stay longer, and if this happens, it means that your hands are hovering on a body part that has a blockage. It means that your energetic field is blocked and that you are tasked to heal it.

5. Be mindful of your breathing. Make sure that you are continuously taking slow and deep breaths. While doing so, hover the palms of your hands once again on top of your head. Smoothly hover your palms as if you are smoothing your hair but without touching your head. Do the same on your face and on the rest of your body. Just hover your palms smoothly as if you are smoothing the wrinkles on the clothes you are wearing.

As you do this, you will feel the strength of Reiki inside your mind and body. Once again, take your time hovering on areas you initially identified as blocked. Be mindful of the various areas of these blockages including their texture, shape, sound, and color. Moreover, be mindful of the places, people, names, and emotions associated to these blockages. Take your time removing these blockages as you replace them with strong Reiki energy.

6. Once again, bring your hands above your head as you continue taking slow and deep breaths. You will once again hover the palms of your hands from one body part to another. However, this time, you are expected to send stronger Reiki energy than the first two times you hovered your hands. This is so because, by this time, the blockages are expected to have been removed or alleviated already.

   As you hover your hands on a body part that you initially identified to have a blockage, take a deep breath then slowly exhale – breathe out not only the air but also the texture, the emotion, the sound, and the color of the blockage.

7. For the last time, allow your hands to go over each body part once again, starting from your head down to your toes. This time, however, you will touch your body parts. Start by touching your head or the location of your crown chakra and then slide your hands down to the back of your head. Then, touch the location of your third eye then move to touch or cover your eyes. Slowly move to cup both of your ears, then cup your cheeks, and then cover your nose and your chin. Make sure that you use both of your hands as you do this.

8. Now, touch the sides of your neck and then slide your hands to your nape or the back of your neck, allowing your fingers to touch. Gently slide your hands to your shoulders then down to your collarbone, to your breastbone, and to your chest. Remember to continuously take slow and deep breaths. Feel the sensation as the Reiki energy flows through the body part you are touching. In this case, feel the sensation of the Reiki energy flowing through your Heart Chakra.

9. From the chest, slide your hands down to your abdomen until you reach the area below your navel. Just like how you did it earlier, continue to take slow and deep breaths and feel the sensation of the Reiki energy flowing through the body part that you are touching. Take your time until you are ready to move on to the next body parts.

10. By this time, you are ready to send Reiki energy to the lower part of your body. You simply have to gently touch each body part, just like how you did it with your upper body.

   Again, your breathing pattern has to be deep and slow. As your hands move from one body part to another, always feel the sensation of the Reiki energy flowing through it. As you exhale, also breathe out any ache and stiffness left from the blockages you earlier identified. As you move to your toes, give each toe a gentle tug. Amazingly feel the sensation as you do this.

11. From your toes, move up to gently touch your elbows as well as your wrists and your fingertips. Just like how you did it to your toes, gently tug each of your fingers. Feel the sensation as you do this.

12. You have gone over each body part at least three times and your next activity now is to basically do the same. However, this time, you are only required to touch body parts that you feel have the need to receive more Reiki energy.

   In some cases, Reiki practitioners experience initially spending more time touching body parts that need additional attention. But as they do this activity, they end up also touching all the other body parts. This is alright as long as you prioritize those that should highly be given attention.

13. By this time, you are expected to feel better and you may already end your session. However, if you feel like

going on and if you want to receive more Reiki energy, feel free to do so by repeating the entire process over and over again until you feel that you have received enough Reiki self-healing.

14. When you are ready to end your session, clasp your hands together and place them in front of your chest. Continue to take deep and slow breaths and continue to feel the healing sensations flowing through your entire body.

15. Continue to take slow and deep breaths and then gently open your eyes as you end your self-healing session.

Reiki Masters suggest their students to always keep a journal of their healing experiences. As for self-healing, it is best that you document your experiences from the time that you conduct your first self-healing session up until the present. That way, you have notes to go back to and you will be able to document the progress you have made.

Conducting self-healing sessions on a daily basis has several benefits for you. First, you are guaranteed to receive consistent healing. Second, the entire session becomes easier and easier to conduct when you do it on a daily basis. That way, you improve and you master your skills in guiding the Reiki energy. Third, you will notice your progress as you feel that the effects of self-healing becomes greater as days pass by.

Step-By-Step Instructions for Self-Healing Meditation (5-10 Minutes)

1. Just like when you conduct a 45-minute self-healing meditation, you have to find a comfortable position before you start the session. You have the option to sit down or lie down. However, in most cases, Reiki practitioners conduct self-healing meditation while sitting down. You have the option to sit on a chair or you may sit Indian-style on the floor.

While lying down may be more comfortable than sitting down, doing the former may cause you to fall asleep. You might end up not completing your meditation session.

For the sake of our discussion, let's agree on doing the Indian-style sit. After all, it is the most ideal and common position among Reiki practitioners.

2. Gently close your eyes and start to take slow and deep breaths. Do this repeatedly until you feel your neck and shoulders softened. Continue doing so until you notice each part of your body relax – from your head to your arms and hands, to your upper body, then down to your hips, your thighs, your knees, your lower legs, your ankles, your feet, and toes. Continue taking slow and deep breaths until you achieve the state of peace and calmness.

3. As you breathe in and breathe out, bring your hands together and start rubbing your palms together. Then, place them on your chest right where you can directly feel your heartbeat. In your most comfortable state, allow Reiki healing to enter your mind and body through the palms of your hands. Allow Reiki to free both your physical and spiritual bodies from any negative force. Once you achieve the state of peace and calmness, it means that you are prepared to start your self-healing session.

4. As soon as you feel the strength of the Reiki energy, you may start your self-healing session by bringing your hands above your head. Make sure that your palms are facing the top of your head. Allow the Reiki energy to enter your head, feel the way it enters and runs through each part of your body until it reaches your toes. Also, be mindful as the energy pass through your heart, your glands, your tissues, and your emotions, among others.

5. From the top of your head, hover your hands down to the sides of your neck and then to your nape. Slide your hands down above the shoulders, the collarbone, and the breastbone. As you hover on your breastbone, your hands should be in a horizontal position, allowing the tip of your middle fingers to touch.

   As you do all these, make sure that you can feel the Reiki energy flowing through you. Also, make sure that you continue to take slow and deep breaths. In the event that you seem to be losing your touch with the Reiki energy, simply start rubbing your palms together again and then go back to where you left off.

6. From the breastbone and down to the chest, slide down your hands to your stomach, down to your abdomen, and then below your navel. Take your time before you hover your hands from one area to another. Again, as you slide your hands from one area to another, your hands must be in a horizontal position, allowing the tip of your middle fingers to touch.

7. Continue to take slow and deep breaths and feel the sensation of the Reiki energy flowing through the body part that you are hovering. Again, in the event that you feel as if you're losing touch with the Reiki energy, simply rub your palms together before you once again proceed with hovering from one body part to the next. Take your time until you are ready to move on to the next body parts.

8. By this time, you are ready to send Reiki energy to the lower part of your body. You simply have to hover each body part, just like how you did it with your upper body.

   Again, your breathing pattern has to be deep and slow. As your hands move from one body part to another, always feel the sensation of the Reiki energy flowing through it.

9. Once you're done, you are required to repeat the entire process but, this time, simply allow your hands to lead and take you to specific parts of your body – or those that need more attention. These specific body parts require you to send more Reiki energy.

   As you pay more attention to these specific body parts, continue to take slow and deep breaths. Breathe in the Reiki energy and breathe out all the aches and stiffness that caused the blockages.

10. When you are ready to end your session, clasp your hands together and place them in front of your chest. Continue to take deep and slow breaths and continue to feel the healing sensations flowing through your entire body.

11. As you breathe in and breathe out, thank Reiki for the successful self-healing experience. Then, gently open your eyes as you end your session.

It's not every day that Reiki practitioners have 45 minutes to spare for self-healing sessions. There are days when we all tend to be busy, leaving us so short a time for daily rituals. That's why shortened sessions are ideal during busy days. However, for beginners, it is advisable to conduct 45-minute sessions. Just like in your case, make sure that you allot at least 45 minutes of your time for this. But once you have mastered your concentration, and that you don't get easily distracted anymore, then that's the time that you may start sessions that last for a maximum of 15 minutes.

At times when Reiki practitioners become exceptionally busy, they perform self-healing for one or two particular body parts only. These are body parts that need healing the most. You can do that too as long as you can assure that you can efficiently put one hundred and one percent concentration on it.

Level 2

In conducting Reiki self-healing Level 2 sessions, expect to still be applying everything you have learned in Reiki self-healing Level 1. The main difference is that you will be applying three additional symbols in Level 2, namely, the Hon Sha Ze Sho Nen symbol, the Sei Hei Ki symbol, and the Choku Rei symbol.

The rule is to basically conduct a Reiki self-healing Level 1 session and then incorporate any of the three additional symbols based on your healing intention. For instance, if your intention is to strengthen your standard Level 1 session, simply apply the Choku Rei symbol, also known as the Power Symbol. This symbol is expected to empower your existing Reiki energy. It provides access to more powerful healing energies.

If you need mental and emotional purification and overall healing, then you must incorporate the Sei Hei Ki symbol in your self-healing session. This symbol focuses on both the conscious and the subconscious minds. It is known as the "mental or emotional healing symbol" but is also regarded by Reiki practitioners as the Protection Symbol. This symbol addresses issues of sufferings and sorrows, and is therefore known to promote both peace and harmony.

If and when you need to address emotional issues, you might have to send healing energies not only to the present moment but also to the past and to the future. This means that you might need to conduct absentee healing and that you will most likely have to send healing energies across time and space. This is when you will be needing the Distance Healing Symbol or the Hon Sha Ze Sho Nen. By incorporating this symbol in your self-healing session, you will not only be able to heal your past but you will also be able to enhance your future.

Chapter 4 Reiki Healing Techniques For Others

Level 1

Level 1 Reiki practitioners do not only have the capability to heal themselves but they are also capable to heal others. All hand positions and healing methods are based on the traditional Usui Reiki techniques. However, it is understandable if you eventually end up applying modified hand positions and techniques. This is expected as you try to adjust based on what works best not only for your client but also for you.

How Should You and Your Client Prepare for a Reiki Healing Level 1 Session?

Before you request your patient to meet you for a Level 1 Reiki Healing session, always make sure that he comes in his most comfortable clothes. You also have to ensure that he is well hydrated before the session starts. It is also best to have a glass of drinking water ready before you start the session just in case you or your patient needs it.

Just like how it is when you conduct a self-healing session, your patient has the option to sit, lie down, or stand during the entire session. The important thing is that he is in his most comfortable state. In most cases, Reiki practitioners request their patients to sit up straight on a chair or to sit Indian-style. Patients used to be requested to lie down as it was also convenient for Reiki practitioners to hover their hand on them. But, unfortunately, majority of the patients tend to fall asleep during the entire session, making it difficult to achieve the maximum level of healing. That's why, nowadays, Reiki practitioners prefer their patients to instead be in a sitting position.

However, before you start your session, ask your patient first about his pre-existing and present health condition. His health might prohibit him from completing the session while standing up or sitting down. Instead, it might be best for him to complete the session while lying down. Moreover, when you have a knowledge of his health condition, you are given an idea as to which body part you are supposed to pay more attention to.

Before the start of the session, your patient may either have his eyes closed or open. There's no specific rule on this. However, in most cases, Reiki practitioners prefer their patients to close their eyes to avoid any kind of distraction.

How Often and How Long Should a Healing Session Be Done?

We have earlier discussed that self-healing must be done on a daily basis to ensure that you receive its maximum benefits. The same is particularly true when you heal others. It is best that you have at least one patient per day. That way, you get to practice healing on a daily basis and you get to master it too in no time. Moreover, you get to monitor your progress if you conduct it on a regular basis.

A healing session may be conducted for a minimum of 30 minutes and a maximum of 90 minutes. The longer the healing session is, the more your patient has to take care of himself. If he has several mental, spiritual, emotional, and physical issues, the session might last for at least an hour or so. This means that you have to instruct him to strictly drink lots of water and be well hydrated before he meets up with you. In the same way that, right after the session, you have to instruct him once again to drink plenty of water and make sure to stay hydrated at all times. Furthermore, he has to avoid drinking alcoholic beverages and caffeine drinks until his mind and body have both adjusted well.

As for how often your patient has to visit you for the healing sessions, the answer is as often as he can. Going to healing sessions is basically the same as going to physical therapy sessions, yoga sessions, or going to the gym – it has to be regularly done to receive the maximum benefits. Most Reiki practitioners require their patients to go to healing sessions for 3 to 4 consecutive days during the first week. In the second week, healing sessions can be lessened to 2 to 3 sessions. Beginning the third week, patients may go to healing sessions 1 to 2 times a week. But then again, it all depends on the severity of your patients' health issues.

What are the Different Hand Positions and Methods for Healing?

The hand techniques and healing approaches used by Reiki practitioners to heal others are, of course, all based on the traditional methods of Usui Reiki. However, there have been modifications on how these hand techniques are done as Reiki practitioners adjust these techniques based on the needs of their patients.

The hand techniques may be done either by slightly touching the patient or by simply hovering your hands over him. In most cases, Reiki practitioners simply hover their hands over each body part of their patients. This is so because there are patients who feel uncomfortable when touched. However, you have the right to ask your patients too of their preference.

For the sake of discussion, let's agree on hovering instead of touching. However, you will learn later on that there are certain healing techniques wherein you don't have a choice but to slightly touch your client. Let's also agree that your patient has his eyes closed and is sitting up straight on a chair.

First Position: Hover Your Hands on Your Patient's Eyes

The first position requires you to hover your hands on the eyes of your patient, with your palms facing downward. This focuses on the Third Eye Chakra and can help heal health issues related to the pineal gland, the pituitary gland, the brain, the sinuses, and the eyes. Among the ailments that this position can cure are flus, colds, allergies, fever, anxiety, and migraine, among others.

As you hover your hands, feel how you send the Reiki healing energy to your patient. If along the way, you find your hands wanting to pay more attention to certain body parts, simply allow your hands to do so and take your time. Do this too for the succeeding hand positions.

Second Position: Hover Your Hands on Your Patient's Temples

The second position requires you to hover your hands on each side of your patient's face, covering the temples and the cheeks. As you do this, include the ears in the scope of this position. Similar to the first position, this also focuses on the Third Eye Chakra and can help heal health issues related to the pineal gland, the pituitary gland, the brain, the sinuses, and the eyes. But this time, it also helps heal health issues related to the ear. Among the illnesses that this position can help cure are flus, allergies, fever, hearing impairment, ear infections, headaches, and eye strain.

Third Position: Cradle Your Patient's Head

In the third position, you don't have a choice but to slightly touch your patient. As you position yourself in front of your client, slip your hands at the back of his head and neck, your fingers intertwined, and your palms touching the sides of his head.

In most cases, when Reiki practitioners perform the third position, their patients tend to fall asleep. This is so because the head and the neck are body parts related to deep rest. If and when you encounter this, don't worry about it. You can continue performing Reiki healing on your patient and he is guaranteed to still receive healing.

Fourth Position: Hover Your Hands on Your Patient's Neck

The fourth position requires you to hover each of your hand on each side of your patient's neck. This focuses on the Throat Chakra and can help heal health issues related to such body parts and organs as the thyroid, vocal chords, lymph nodes, pulmonary arteries, esophagus, and lungs. Among the diseases that it can cure are laryngitis, asthma, heart and artery problems, thyroid diseases, and lymphatic disorders. This position also addresses communication issues including the fear of speaking in public.

Fifth Position: Hover Your Hands on Your Patient's Sternum or Breastbone

The fifth position requires you to hover your hands on your patient's sternum, also known as the breastbone which is located below the collarbone. This focuses on the Heart Chakra and can help heal health issues related to different body parts and organs including the breasts, the thymus gland, the heart, and the upper lungs. Among the illnesses it can cure or alleviate are breast cancer, heart problems, pneumonia, asthma, and other health issues related to breathing. It also helps address anxiety, chronic stress, and other issues related to love, self-love, and any form of relationships.

Sixth Position: Hover Your Hands on Your Patient's Chest

The sixth position requires you to hover your hands on the chest of your patient, or the area right below your collarbone and above your stomach. This also focuses on the Heart Chakra and further heals or alleviates health issues that can be addressed in the fifth position.

Seventh Position: Hover Your Hands on Your Patient's Stomach

The seventh position requires you to hover your hands on the stomach of your patient. This focuses on the Solar Plexus Chakra and can help heal health issues related to different body parts and organs including the liver, the gallbladder, the kidneys, the pancreas, and the stomach. Among the ailments that this position can help cure or alleviate are kidney diseases, liver diseases, and illnesses related to the digestive tract. If your patient lacks inspiration to work or to live in general, this is the position that can help address such issue as the Solar Plexus Chakra is connected to creativity.

Eighth Position: Hover Your Hands Between Your Patient's Navel and Groin

The eighth position requires you to hover your hands below your patient's stomach but above the groin. This allows you to perform healing on different body parts and organs such as the colon, and the large and small intestines. This position further heals or alleviates health issues described in the seventh position. At the same time, it also heals and alleviates bowel problems.

Ninth Position: Hover Your Hands on Your Patient's Groin

The ninth position requires you to hover your hands on your patient's groin. The health issues that this position can help cure or alleviate include digestive tract problems, urinary tract problems, pregnancy issues, hormonal problems, and illnesses related to the reproductive system, among others. This position focuses on the Root Chakra which means that this also addresses financial, safety, and security issues.

Tenth Position: Hover Your Hands on Your Patient's Legs

The tenth position requires you to hover your hands on each of your patient's legs. Send Reiki healing energy from the hips down to the soles of his feet. Some Reiki practitioners tend to gently tug the heels of their patients' feet. You may do the same too. A little stretching of the legs help bring more energy in your patient.

Performing Hand Positions and Healing Techniques on Both Sides of the Body

You have to ensure that you perform Reiki healing on all body parts and organs. In most cases, Reiki practitioners perform healing by going over both sides of their patient's body to ensure that they do not miss a body part. They also generally believed that doing so further strengthens healing.

If your patient is lying down on his back, ask him to roll and lie on his stomach so you can perform the same hand positions and healing techniques on the other side of his body. If your patient is sitting down, it is easier to perform healing for the other side of the body. However, you have to instruct him to stand up when you are about to hover your hands on his buttocks and at the back of his thighs. If your patient is standing up, all the more that it is easier to perform healing on both sides.

Level 2

When performing Level 2 Reiki Healing, you will highly need the three additional Reiki symbols, namely, the Choku Rei, the Sei Hei Ki, and the Hon Sha Ze Sho Nen. This is so because healing Level 2 patients means exerting more effort for their intensive physical healing and emotion healing. Furthermore, if your patient is unable to physically visit you for a healing session, you will have to doubly perform healing that includes the Hon Sha Ze Sho Nen symbols, especially if healing requires you to learn his past and his future.

Don't forget that Level 2 Reiki Healing does not mean that you only get to apply the three Reiki symbols. Always remember that you can still perform the Level 1 Reiki healing techniques and hand position, and incorporate one, two, or all Reiki symbols in it to further strengthen your Reiki Healing capabilities. For instance, if your intention is to strengthen your standard Level 1 healing session, simply apply the Choku Rei symbol, also known as the Power Symbol. This symbol is expected to empower your existing Reiki energy. It provides access to more powerful healing energies. The Choku Rei symbol can help further heal or alleviate terminal sickness, injuries, surgeries, and other chronic health problems.

If you need mental and emotional purification and overall healing, then you must incorporate the Sei Hei Ki symbol in your healing session. This symbol focuses on both the conscious and the subconscious minds. It is known as the "mental or emotional healing symbol" but is also regarded by Reiki practitioners as the Protection Symbol. This symbol addresses issues of sufferings and sorrows, and is therefore known to promote both peace and harmony.

If and when you need to address emotional issues of your patient, you might have to send healing energies not only to the present moment but also to the past and to the future. This means that you might need to conduct absentee healing and that you will most likely have to send healing energies across time and space. This is when you will be needing the Distance Healing Symbol or the Hon Sha Ze Sho Nen. By incorporating this symbol in your healing session, you will not only be able to heal your past but you will also be able to enhance your future.

Of course, aside from having to send healing energies across time and space, there are also instances in which your patient can't be physically present to receive Reiki healing – in which case, you also need to conduct Distance Healing. There are, in fact, two traditional approaches to Distance Healing, namely, the Surrogate Approach and the Thigh and Knee Approach.

Distance Healing: The Surrogate Approach

In applying the Surrogate Approach, you need to use an object that will serve as the substitute of your patient. You may use any object so long as you can effectively channel Reiki through it. The common objects being used include crystals, teddy bears, dolls, cushions, a photograph, and you – yes, you can also be the patient's surrogate. In most cases though, a doll is used to practice the Surrogate Approach. This is so because a doll is basically patterned after the physical appearance of a human being, and so it's easier to do the healing session using it.

You must remember that before the healing session begins, you must first make it clear to yourself and to Reiki that the object you are using is merely a substitute to a particular patient. To conduct the healing session per se, you basically perform the hand positions and healing approaches you use when you heal a person face-to-face. However, you might have to increase your level of concentration when doing this approach because of the physical absence of your patient. This means that you might also have to increase the level of your imagination to ensure the effectiveness of sending Reiki energies to your patient. This is why it is advisable to conduct Distance Healing in a private place or any location where you won't easily get distracted.

Distance Healing: The Thigh and Knee Approach

You will be required to sit down when you perform the Thigh and Knee Approach. Just like when you use the Surrogate Approach, you will also need to increase the level of your imagination to make your healing session an effective one.

Once seated comfortably, touch your right knee and right thigh using your right hand. Imagine that your right knee is the head of your patient and your right thigh is his entire body. Then, touch your left knee and your left thigh, imagine them to be the back of your patient's head and the back of his body, respectively. With full concentration, make it clear to yourself and to Reiki that your knees and your thighs will serve as the substitute of your patient and that you will perform healing using them. To start, simply apply the hand positions and healing approaches that you apply when you perform Reiki healing on your patient fact-to-face.

SENDING REIKI ENERGIES TO HEAL RELATIONSHIPS

Have you ever heard of that old love song, "Why Do We Always Hurt the Ones We Love?" by Dan Hill? Well, you don't even have to know the entire lyrics of the song. By simply reading the title, you already know that there is truth in it.

We always thought that life would be easy and flawless if we live with people we love and people who love us just as much.

But, in reality, life doesn't become easy because of love. Instead, you get inspired and motivated to live your life because of the people you love and the people who love you despite of all the hardships in life. Hurting them is unavoidable because we are different individuals that way. You think differently from others, you understand things differently from others, you expect others to do things that did not even enter their minds, and vice versa. All these, of course, result to miscommunication that eventually lead to misunderstandings, hatred, and anger.

The sad part is that even though you tell yourself that you have forgiven the people who have hurt you, you still feel some negative emotions deep inside you. Then, of course, there are times when you also find yourself having a difficult time forgiving people and you end up hating them forever. Well, through Reiki healing, all negativity can be transformed using the Universe's healing vibrations. Through Reiki healing, you will be able to create and re-create beautiful relationships – be it with your significant others, or with your family, relatives, and friends.

A Reiki self-healing session to heal relationships may be done by using the techniques applied in performing distance healing. You must also incorporate the Cho Ku Rei healing symbol in order to further strengthen your Reiki healing power. When performing the session, you must talk to yourself loudly and verbally express your emotional issues. That way, it will be clear as to which issues need Reiki healing.

You must also be aware that healing relationships don't necessarily mean that all ill relationships will be fixed in such a way that you will then be reunited with someone. You must anticipate that some relationships might have to permanently end in order for healing to take place. Apparently, what's being removed are the negative emotions deep inside you as well as all the negative emotions residing on the people you have conflict with.

Step-by-Step Instructions to Heal Relationships through Reiki

1. Find a comfortable position before you begin the session. However, the most recommended one is sitting up straight either on a comfortable chair or on the floor doing the Indian-style sit.

2. Gently close both of your eyes and do some deep breathing exercises to allow your mind and body to relax.

3. Bring your hands together and do the Gassho position. Clear your mind and condition yourself that you are about to begin a Reiki healing session. Open your mind and body as they allow the Reiki energy to flow inside you.

4. With your eyes closed, feel the way the Reiki energy enters your Crown Chakra and eventually run through every part of your body.

5. Still with your eyes closed, make sure that your internal gaze is focused between your eyebrows or right where your Third Eye is positioned.

6. As you keep your internal gaze on your Third Eye, create a mental image of the person that you have a conflict with.

7. As you look at that person using the mental image you have created, identify the Reiki symbols covering his mind and body.

8. Create a mental image of you standing in front of him, and then, identify the Reiki symbols covering your mind and body this time.

9. Now, create a mental image of you approaching him and giving him a big hug. Utter kind and loving words to him. You must be mindful that everything you say to him are good and positive things only. You must also

make sure that you feel in your heart the truthfulness of each word you say. Doing so will help you improve your feelings towards that person from negative to positive.

10. Continuously keep your internal gaze on your Third Eye. Then, create an ideal mental image of how you want your relationship with this person to eventually turn out to be. For instance, if the other person is your spouse, you may create a mental image of you and him living together in a harmonious manner. Imagine that the Universe's purest light is radiating upon the two of you.

11. Identify the Reiki symbols that represent your harmonious relationship. As you continuously create a mental image of your harmonious relationship with the other person, add the Reiki symbols in that image. For example, if your mental image indicates you and him hugging each other, allow the Reiki symbol or symbols to appear on top your image together. It's basically similar to adding a text above an image or a photo.

12. Concentrate on the mental image that you have created which, of course, includes the Reiki symbols you have added. Do not lose your mental image of it. Continue your concentration until you feel your inner self tell you that you are ready to end your meditation session.

13. Once you feel ready to end the session, start rubbing your palms together then place each palm on each of your eyes. Feel the heat that your palms bring to your eyes. Put down your hands and gently open both of your eyes.

14. You are advised to do this healing session consistently on a daily basis. In fact, you may conduct this as many times as you want in one day. The important thing is that you feel better each time you conduct the session.

Healing the relationship doesn't happen overnight that's why you are recommended to consistently perform the session on a daily basis. That way, you get to constantly believe that you have a wonderful relationship with the person whom you have a conflict with. It's basically like applying the law of attraction to improve your relationship with that person.

As earlier mentioned, healing a relationship doesn't necessarily mean being reunited with that person or bringing back your closeness to each other. Healing a relationship may also mean letting that person go and letting him choose his own path. In other words, healing a relationship may also mean moving on with or without that person. The important thing is that the negative emotions that you used to have for each other will be gone and healed.

The instructions for performing a Reiki session on a patient to heal his relationship with another person are basically the same. It's just that, apparently, you are performing the session for another person. In doing so, you have to guide your patient until he learns to forgive the person whom he has a conflict with. He has to meet you on a regular basis to make the Reiki healing effective.

SENDING REIKI ENERGIES TO ATTRACT TRUE LOVE

In this section, let's first discuss the seven chakras and how each of them has a role to play in finding your one true love.

1. The Root Chakra

The first chakra helps you get grounded. It helps you maintain your calmness and your self-awareness. When you have a healthy Root Chakra, you will surely find true love with ease and grace.

2. The Sacral Chakra

The second chakra focuses on searching for your magnetic presence. An active and healthy Sacral Chakra goes searching for the energy of others as you use up your own energy. There is a tendency for you to feel drained because the energy of others will flow through you. However, with effective meditation, you will be able to prevent yourself from draining too much energy.

The ideal time to make the Sacral Chakra active is during intimate moments with the other person or when you are alone.

3. The Solar Plexus Chakra

The third chakra brings out the extrovert in you. An active Solar Plexus Chakra allows you to confidently look for and go out on dates until you find your true love. You will even find yourself being active in using dating sites. At the same time, you will find yourself asking your friends to set you up on dates. Moreover, you will find yourself doing enjoyable activities that will give you the chance to find your true love.

4. The Heart Chakra

The fourth chakra focuses on self-love. The love that you will receive will all depend on the love that you give to yourself. For instance, if you lack self-love, this will reflect on your relationship. In other words, the love that you will receive is based on the love that you deserve which is based on how you love yourself.

If you want to find true love, be truthful to how you love yourself too. Love yourself the way you want to be loved. Trust yourself that way you want to be trusted. If you believe you deserve to receive overflowing love from your significant other, then you first have to receive overflowing love from yourself.

5. The Throat Chakra

The fifth chakra focuses on being true to yourself. Sometimes, when a person's trying so hard to look for a significant other, the tendency is for that person to have pretensions. He becomes conscious of how he looks. He tries to live in an ideal but fake world. He becomes untruthful not only to his significant other but, most especially, to himself.

With a healthy and active Throat Chakra, you get to freely express yourself and you learn to live without any pretension. That way, you get to act in a comfortable manner. When you are comfortable with your own self, chances are that you will find a man who will feel comfortable with you.

6. The Third Eye Chakra

The sixth chakra focuses on knowing your own worth. If you know your own worth, you know which type of person to attract. For instance, if you have so many negative things to say to yourself such as, "I've already accepted the fact that I will live alone" or "I'm not good enough for anybody" or "I'm ugly that's why nobody gets attracted to me," well, chances are that you will either not find a significant other or you will attract a person who will end up to be a difficult person.

So, when you have a healthy and active Third Eye, then you are expected to be a person filled with positivity inside yourself and you very well know your self-worth. You know your value as a person and will not settle for someone less than you deserve. You will gain your confidence, reminding yourself that someday you will find the right person for you.

7. The Crown Chakra

The seventh chakra focuses on manifesting the love that you want to attract. This chakra will connect you to spirituality and provide you the power to express the love that you desire to receive.

To sum it all up, healthy and active chakras basically tell you that if you have an ideal man or woman in your mind, you will undoubtedly end up with that person only if you also have the characteristics you are looking for in him or her. Have you ever heard of that adage, "whatever your heart and mind can conceive, you will achieve"? In all honesty, that adage absolutely have a truth in it.

Sending Reiki Energy to Attract Your Soul Mate

If you are wondering if there is some truth about having a soul mate, well the answer to that is, yes, your soul mate exists. Each one of us has a soul mate. There will always be someone who will match your personality, and if you are getting impatient about meeting that person, well, all you need is a lot more patience. Most importantly, you have to put your one hundred percent trust in the divine timing.

The Capability of Reiki to Clear Out Old Energies

Reiki healing is not only capable of helping you find your soul mate, but it is also capable of allowing you to let go of relationship patterns that don't seem to do you any good. Sometimes, you also feel as if you have already moved on from your past relationships but, actually, you haven't. Through Reiki healing, you get to realize these things and help you move on in its truest sense. That way, when you find yourself wanting to enter into a new relationship, you will have a different approach this time. You will stop applying the old relationship patterns that formed part of your life and, more than anything else, you will stop encountering the same old relationship problems that you kept on encountering over and over again.

Completely letting go of old relationship patterns will enable you to fine tune yourself and eventually become a better version of yourself. Once you let go of the old and negative patterns, you will eventually have space for new Reiki energies. Fill this space with positivity. Fill it with energies that will allow you to manifest love, empowerment, communication, and all other good and positive qualities that will allow you to connect with the divine self.

The Capability of Reiki to Help You Enjoy Being Single

Reiki healing is also capable of helping you learn how to have fun even if you're single. Reiki will help you have a better relationship with yourself. Through Reiki healing, you will learn to love yourself the way you want others to love you. Once you master this, you will not get impatient anymore when it comes to waiting for your one true love. This is so because you learn to enjoy being single that you already feel complete just by being with yourself. You achieve a deeper relationship with yourself which will eventually allow you to have a deeper relationship with your significant other once you find him or her.

The Capability of Reiki to Help You Bolster Trust and Patience

Reiki healing is also capable of honing your patience and trust in the so-called divine timing. In most cases, this transpires after letting go of all negativity and replacing them with new Reiki energies but you still haven't found your soul mate or your significant other. If and when this happens to you, remind yourself that there is this so-called divine timing.

Are you familiar of the adage that goes something like, "Sometimes, you find exactly what you're looking for where you least expect it"? Well, there's a truth behind that adage, be it about love or something else. This is true because you don't express any resistance to the thought of meeting the right person for you.

SENDING REIKI ENERGIES TO HELP CLEAR FINANCIAL BLOCKS

There are three processes that will generally help you clear financial blocks. First, you need to identify the limiting beliefs that you have concerning money. Second, you need to release those limiting beliefs. Lastly, you need to replace those limiting beliefs with new and more positive beliefs concerning money. These processes may be executed with or without Reiki. If you can successfully do this without the help of Reiki, then good for you. However, doing so might be quite a challenge. Thankfully, there is Reiki healing that can help you become more disciplined and more motivated to strictly follow these processes. In this section, let's discuss each of these processes by providing step-by-step instructions on how to execute them.

Identify the Limiting Beliefs that You Have Concerning Money

- Find a comfortable position and a conducive place to conduct your Reiki self-healing session. Again, it doesn't matter if you are standing up, sitting down, or lying down, as long as you are comfortable in that position. However, standing up is generally the least comfortable position there is and you might end up getting tired and, worse, you might end up losing your concentration. Lying down may be the most comfortable position – so comfortable that you might end up falling asleep and, sadly, you might not be able to finish the session. As mentioned in the previous sections, sitting up straight is still the most recommended position in which you have the option to either sit on the chair or on the floor doing the Indian-style sit.

- Prepare a pen and a piece of paper as you will need to eventually write down something. Just place them beside you.

- You have the option to either close your eyes or open your eyes – whichever is more comfortable and convenient for you. The important thing is that you don't lose your concentration.

- Start taking slow and deep breaths to make you feel more comfortable and relaxed. Continuously do this until the end of the session.

- Recall as far back as your childhood years and try your best to remember the first time you learned about money and its use. In general, it is more convenient and effective to recall such memories with your eyes closed. However, this is not a strict rule.

- If you seem to be having a difficult time recalling this, do not get frustrated because this happens to all beginners. All you have to do is to sit and wait until a vague recollection of it surfaces. Once this happens, that vague recollection will eventually become vivid memories. Eventually, the next time you conduct this type of healing session, you will not have a hard time recalling this anymore.

- Now, evaluate the memories that came to your mind. Are these memories positive or negative?

- Reach for your pen and paper, and then, jot down all the memories that entered your mind.

- Remember that the memories don't have to be during your childhood years only. You only have to go all the way back to your younger years so that you will avoid missing any important recollection. If you recall limiting beliefs that only came up when you had your first job, make sure to jot it down. If you suddenly realize that just a few weeks ago, you unconsciously came up with a limiting belief, jot it down too. Write down everything that you think is related to the topic. It may be about your limiting beliefs but, this time, don't limit yourself at all.

Release Those Limiting Beliefs

- After jotting them all down, perform Reiki healing for each and every memory. Take your time in sending Reiki healing. Don't limit yourself of the time. Continue performing the healing session for each memory until you feel good and satisfied. That means that you have successfully released and healed the money issue residing deep inside you.

- It helps to replay each and every memory in your head and then imagine how you would have instead wanted it to happen. For instance, during your childhood years, you were told by your parents that the money they earned were not sufficient to raise a family. Apparently, such statement established your belief that working did not mean that you would eventually become rich. Counter such belief by telling yourself, with conviction, that you don't deserve to earn low and that you will always earn enough money for yourself and for your family. This is what we call positive affirmations and allowing yourself to absorb such positive beliefs brings about reassurance, relief, and love. Do bear in mind to consistently allow yourself to experience positive beliefs and emotions.

- As you think of these positive beliefs and emotions, simultaneously send Reiki energy to further strengthen positivity.

Replace Those Limiting Beliefs with New and More Positive Beliefs Concerning Money

- By this time, you have not only successfully identified the money blocks residing inside you but you have released them as well. In this last process, you will have to replace your negative money beliefs with positive ones. In fact, you have already started doing this in the second process. In this third process, however, your task is to further strengthen your positive beliefs and create more of them.

- Start by imagining how you would like your life to turn out in two years' time. Create mental images that are as vivid as possible. For instance, imagine that after two years, you have saved and invested enough money for your retirement. Imagine that you have a way better life after two years. You can now afford to travel in other countries at least twice a year. You can provide more than enough for your family.

  You are recommended to create mental images as specific as possible. For instance, envision yourself having a net worth of one million U.S. dollars in two years' time. Envision yourself to own a beautiful house in Beverly Hills, California. Envision yourself free of any debt.

- Make sure that you apply all your five senses when you envision these things – your sense of sight, sense of touch, sense of smell, sense of taste, and sense of hearing. That way, you ultimately feel deep inside you everything that you envision. If you feel it, it's like you're claiming that, indeed, it will all come true.

- Make sure that as you create mental images of what you want to achieve in two years' time, you also visualize how it will all happen. Don't entertain negative thoughts such as "My thoughts seem idealistic" or "Should I make my thoughts more realistic?" Simply visualize in full detail everything that you want to achieve. Visualize how you will make them all happen.

- Make sure that as you visualize how you will make each of your goals happen, you are not incorporating activities that will do harm to other people because doing so is a negative act. Always bear in mind that you are to do positive things only to make it all happen. For instance, don't envision yourself getting promoted at work because you pulled someone else down. Instead, envision yourself getting promoted because you proposed and executed projects that contributed to the long-term growth of the company.

- Send Reiki energy to each of the things you have envisioned for a minimum of 10 minutes. Take your time in sending Reiki energy. Do not rush and just enjoy the moment.

- When you feel you are prepared to end your Reiki healing session, continue to take slow and deep breaths as you open your eyes – if they are closed – and be thankful for the session.

- To ensure the effectiveness of Reiki healing, conduct a session on a daily basis.

After conducting a few sessions, it is normal to find yourself recalling more limiting beliefs which did not resurface during your first few sessions. This happens to anybody. If and when you encounter this, simply repeat the three process for that particular limiting belief.

Once you have mastered conducting this type of Reiki healing on yourself, you are then prepared to conduct sessions for others. This can be a one-on-one session with your patient or you can conduct this as a group. As a matter of fact, a group session is highly recommended because it is during this time that the Reiki energy level is higher. This is so because everyone participating in the group session is seeking to achieve a common goal – to remove financial blocks.

SENDING REIKI ENERGIES TO TRANSFORM NEGATIVE EXPERIENCES INTO POSITIVE ONES

Sometimes in life, you get caught up in negative situations that seem to be irresolvable. It's as if you want to give up on life. If and when you experience feeling this way, quickly remind yourself that Reiki can help you feel better. Remind yourself that Reiki can help you transform negative situations into positive ones. All you need to do is believe in its healing power.

Below is the step-by-step instructions for conducting a Reiki self-healing session that would help in solving difficult situations:

- Sit comfortably on a chair or Indian-style on the floor. Make sure that you are sitting up straight and that you are not slouching.

- Start taking slow and deep breaths to make you feel more comfortable and relaxed. Continuously do this until the end of the session.

- Once you feel relaxed and comfortable, you may start your Reiki self-healing session.

- Put your hands together and bring them to the Gassho position. Clear your mind and heart, and welcome the Reiki energy to enter through your Crown Chakra and flow through every part of your body.

- Gently close both of your eyes as you continue to feel the way the Reiki energy is running through your mind and body.

- With your eyes closed, place your internal gaze where your Third Eye is positioned – which is right between your eyebrows.

- Then, visualize a blackboard as you continue to internally gaze between your eyebrows. As you look at the blackboard, you see all the negative situations that you are in. This will naturally cause negative emotions to turn up. Whatever emotions come up, don't hold back. Allow yourself to feel them.

- Now, visualize yourself reaching for an eraser and wiping off everything you saw on the blackboard. Then, replace those negative images with positive ones. Create mental images of how you want the negative situations to be solved. Create a genuinely positive mental images or images that create joy, love, harmony, and all other positive emotions. As you visualize this, incorporate a bright purple light surrounding the images.

- Then, visualize yourself writing Reiki symbols on top of the mental images you have created. For instance, on the blackboard, you are visualizing yourself laughing with your spouse, imagine yourself placing a Reiki symbol on top of that image.

- Make the positive mental images you have created as vivid as possible in such a way that it will be easy for you to retain the images in your head. Then, every time your problems or the negative situations enter your mind, quickly think of those positive mental images to prevent yourself from feeling anxious or from worrying. Don't forget to always include the Reiki symbols in your mental images.

- Take your time in replacing the negative images with strong positive images. Make sure to include every negative thing that causes your stress and anxiety. Then, ensure that you also replace all of them with positive images.

- As soon as you're ready to end your Reiki self-healing session, rub your palms together and then gently place each palm on each of your eyes. Feel the heat that your palms bring to your eyes. Then, when you're ready, gently put down your hands and open both of your eyes.

- Perform this Reiki self-healing session on a daily basis until all your negative situations have completely changed into positive ones. You can conduct the session as often as you want in one day. The important thing is that every time you conduct a session, it never fails to make you feel better. If, along the way, you feel impatient as if your problems are not being solved, you are advised to simply perform a Reiki self-healing session to feel better. Simply trust the process and don't ever doubt the power of Reiki to ensure its effectiveness.

Once you have mastered conducting this type of Reiki healing on yourself, you are then prepared to conduct sessions for others. This can be a one-on-one session with your patient or you can conduct this as a group. As a matter of fact, a group session is highly recommended because it is during this time that the Reiki energy level is higher. This is so because everyone participating in the group session is seeking to achieve a common goal – to replace all negative situations into positive ones.

Ask your patients to undergo this type of Reiki healing session with you as often as possible to achieve desired results as soon as possible. Having a session on a daily basis is, of course, the most recommended one. But if your patient's schedule doesn't permit him to visit you every day, then encourage him to have a session every other day during his first week. In the second week, you may ask him to have a session with you at least three times. In the third week, he can come to see you for a session twice. That way, you still get to send him Reiki energies on a regular basis.

By the time he reaches the third week of sessions, he is expected to have already become familiar of the entire healing process. This means that he may start conducting meditation sessions at home all by himself.

SENDING REIKI ENERGIES TO ATTRACT EVERYTHING THAT YOU DESIRE TO HAVE

The Reiki self-healing session that will help you attract everything you want in life is basically the same as the other sessions earlier discussed in this book. However, the difference lies on the fact that before you start the session, you have to make sure that you already have a ready list of the things you want to achieve. However, your list should be written in such a way that they seem to be happening at the present time. For instance, instead of listing your wishes this way:

1. I will be hired by a prestigious company.

2. I will soon have enough money.

3. I will soon have my own car.

You should list them this way:

1. I am currently working at a prestigious financial services company.

2. I am thankful to have earned one million U.S. dollars today.

3. I am currently driving my own Maserati.

While you are recommended to be as specific as possible when listing down the things that you desire to have, there are some limitations to it too. First, never mention specific names of people. For instance, if your wish is to finally meet your future significant other, don't write down, "I am meeting Scarlett Johansson today" or "I am meeting Chris Hemsworth today" – or don't write the name of your co-worker and whoever your crush is. Instead, write down the qualities that you are looking for in a person that you would want to be with for the rest of your life. For example, you may write, "Today, I'm dating a beautiful and intelligent person who likes me just as much as I like her," or something like, "Today, I'm meeting a person who's a good conversationalist, who has a good sense of humor, and who likes me just as much as I do towards him."

In the same way that you're not supposed to specify the name of the company that you would like to work for. Instead, write down the qualities of the company that you're interested to apply in. For instance, you're not supposed to write, "I'm working at XYZ Corp." but rather, "I'm working at a multinational consumer goods company."

Here are the step-by-step instructions for conducting a Reiki session that will help you attract everything that you desire to have:

- On a piece of paper, jot down everything that you wish to have based on the tips given earlier.

- Then, create a vivid mental image of each of the items on your list.

- Perform an aura cleansing exercise and a meditation or a spiritual session based on the step-by-step instructions discussed in the previous sections.

- Then, with your eyes closed, recall the vivid mental images that you created in your mind right before you started the aura cleansing exercise and the meditation session. Make sure that your mental images unfold as if they are happening in real life. Make your images seem as real as possible.

- While the mental images are in your mind, imagine them transpiring while enclosed in the rays of light. Imagine them glowing brightly.

- Then, write the applicable Reiki symbols on top of each image in your mind. Notice how the positive emotions strengthen right after indicating the Reiki symbols. Enjoy the positive emotions that you feel.

- Keep those positive emotions inside you. Don't let any negative emotion get in the way because it will badly affect your goal of achieving everything you desire to have.

- Continuously do this session until you have fully strengthened both your mental images and your positive emotions. Make the images and emotions so strong that even in normal days, you can easily create vivid and positive thoughts anywhere you may be.

- In doing this session, you will observe that your power here is your emotion. If and when you think of the mental images, it is supposed to consistently make you feel good. This session apparently greatly incorporates the law of attraction.

Chapter 5 Ideal Foods and Drinks for Your Chakras

In Chapter 1, it was mentioned how eating fruits and vegetables can ultimately help you achieve effective Reiki healing sessions. Such topic shall be further discussed in this chapter, along with many other related sub-topics.

Just like any other beliefs that people have, the beliefs of Reiki practitioners about Reiki have also experienced evolution over the years. In the past, Reiki practitioners thought that in order for the Universal Life Energy to be connected to them, all they needed was to attend Reiki classes for students and then receive attunements. However, further research indicate that there are indeed various levels of effectiveness, various levels of strengths, and various levels of vibrations that a Reiki practitioner has to be knowledgeable of. Such variations are composed of several kinds of factors, emotions, or feelings such as joy, love, compassion, calmness, relaxation, and peace, among many others.

As mentioned, such factors or emotions have different levels and, apparently, there will be circumstances when you need to possess higher healing energies lest you drain yourself mentally, physically, and emotionally. This only means that your human body has to have the capability to channel different frequencies and different levels of vibrations. If your body is not in good shape or you have poor health, chances are that your Reiki practice might not become effective. This is the time when you'll realize that you have to take good care of your health, and what better way to practice this but by eating the right kinds of food – and drinks for that matter.

In the succeeding sections, you will learn which food are good for you and which are not.

SUGAR

There are different kinds of sugar. The major ones are known as maltose or malt sugar, glucose or the sugar found in your blood, dextrose or the glucose found in corn, fructose or the sugar found in fruits, and sucrose or what is commonly known as table sugar. There's also honey that apparently has sugar content.

You will determine your sugar level through the glycemic index (GI), which is the basis of the impact of food on your blood sugar. A high GI in the food you consume means that your blood sugar level is mostly likely to skyrocket and then would drastically decline soon thereafter. Whereas, a low GI in the food you consume means that there will be a slow increase in your blood sugar level. A high GI will cause your body to have a difficult time maintaining its stability. In most cases, the common illnesses related to a high GI include hypoglycemia, diabetes, and illnesses related to the pancreas. However, there are research indicating that a high GI also causes immune system suppression, fertility issues, and cognitive dysfunction.

Immune System Suppression

Several research findings indicate that glucose indeed has a negative impact on our immune system. In one of the studies conducted, mice with tumors were used as study subjects in which one group consumed foods with a high level of sucrose and the other group consumed foods without any sucrose. The results indicated that those that consumed food with sucrose did not produce enough T-cells and their tumors were noticeably larger.

A research on the impact of glucose on leukocytes, also known as white blood cells, was also studied in early 1960s. The leukocytes have the capability of shielding the human body from diseases by destroying undesirable organisms found in a human's blood stream. In the said study, it was revealed that each leukocyte of a person who did not consume any sugar for approximately 12 hours could destroy 14 undesirable organisms. On the contrary, the leukocytes of a person who ate a slice of cake would weaken and could only eliminate 1 bacteria. Unfortunately, such occurrence could definitely weaken the immune system which would then have an impact on your aura and be prone to psychological and psychic issues. Evidently, the key to improve your health is to totally ban yourself from consuming anything with sugar in it.

Fertility Issues

Several research findings reveal that a person who eats food with sugar, carbohydrates, and a high level of GI is more likely to become infertile than a person who doesn't consume food with such content. The results of a study indicated that women who consumed food with high glycemic-load had more than 90 percent chances of experiencing ovulatory infertility compared to women who consumed food with low or no glycemic-load. There are various kinds of food that can enhance ovulation or the chances of a woman to get pregnant. Among these are whole fruits, vegetables, beans, and whole grains.

Cognitive Dysfunction

The results of several studies on the impact of glucose on a person's cognitive health indicate that a person's high consumption of refined sugar could result in a decline in mental function level. In one research, more than 60 children with ages ranging between 6 and 11 years old participated as study subjects. For several days, the children were instructed to eat a low GI cereal for breakfast and some other days they consumed a high GI cereal for breakfast. When they took memory and attention tests every morning after breakfast, it was found that memory performance was lower after eating the high GI cereal.

This goes to show that people should increase their intake of foods with low GI as it will provide a sufficient amount of glucose that would enable a person to augment his mental function and successfully make it through the day.

Having discussed these 3 illnesses, you'll definitely have an idea that sugar indeed has a negative impact on your health. A fluctuating blood glucose level means unstable spiritual, mental, emotional, and physical health. Unfortunately, such occurrence would hinder you from handling Reiki energies with high frequencies. Minimizing your sugar intake will allow you to effectively perform Reiki teaching, attunements, and treatments.

It is highly recommended though that if you want this health issue addressed, you have to stop your sugar intake one hundred percent. This is so because it's more difficult to stop the habit if you gradually do it. Completely eliminating sugar from your life would eventually eliminate your desire for sweets. This is contrary to simply reducing your sugar intake – this will only encourage you to crave for sweets.

Are artificial substitutes to sugar recommended? Well, the answer is no. Such substitutes as sorbitolorxylitol, acesulfame potassium, neotame, sucralose, aspartame, saccharin, and the like, are not recommended too. Because these are not the real kind, the human body gets confused on how to react to these substitutes. In other words, you better start practicing not to consume sugar and to not even try substitutes.

CHOCOLATE

The chocolate has 3 chemical contents that are harmful for Reiki practitioners, namely, phenylethylamine, theobromine, and sugar. As previously discussed, sugar is detrimental to the health of Reiki practitioners. The glucose has the frightening ability of quickly elevating to the brain and quickly dropping as well which result in an unstable brain chemistry. In general, people think that sugar consumption could make them feel better – they could work more efficiently, they would become more motivated to work, and so on. However, this could be true only at the start. Sooner or later, they would feel too exhausted to think and move.

The theobromine chemical content found in the chocolate forms part of the caffeine family. It negatively impacts the neurotransmitters found in the nervous system which then creates imbalance and causes mood swings.

The Phenylethylamine chemical content augments the dopamine levels of the brain. It also has an impact on the changes in the brain chemistry. An imbalanced amount of phenylethylamine in the body would also result in an imbalanced mind and body.

People in general have the wrong notion that if they eat chocolate, it would make their mind and body more active and more inspired to work. Perhaps, there's some truth to that because, in most cases, if you eat a piece of chocolate, it seems as if you become more energized. However, this is only temporary as its chemical content would eventually cause imbalances in your nervous system. This, unfortunately, will hinder your capability to connect to a higher Reiki energy.

MEAT

This kind of food includes turkey, chicken, pork, and beef, among others, which, when consumed, is heavy in the stomach. In general, they are not considered healthy food because turkeys, chickens, pigs, and cows are apparently not in a naturally healthy condition when slaughtered. Of course, the distress, anger, and fear that they felt while being slaughtered would reflect on the condition of their bodies. Just imagine yourself eating a piece of chicken that felt distressed while being killed. The negative content in it would most likely be passed on to you. Moreover, this kind of food most likely contains chemicals resulting from antibiotics, pesticides, and other harmful substances that had to be used during the meat production process. These negative contents found in turkey, chicken, pork, beef, and the like, can terribly hinder the way you channel your Reiki energy.

This is the reason why health conscious people prefer to eat fish. Fish is not difficult to digest compared to meat and doesn't encounter similar psychic burden like the one encountered by turkeys, chickens, pigs, and cows. Aside from that, fish is good for the cardiovascular system and also consists of omega oils that may contribute to relaxation. However, not all fishes are healthy as there are those with high mercury content such as tuna particularly the canned albacore and steaks, tilefish particularly the golden snapper, swordfish, shark, sea bass, pike, oysters, king mackerel, and the Atlantic halibut.

Those that have low mercury content include sturgeon, striped bass, clams, farmed catfish, Pacific salmon, wild Alaska salmon, tilapia, Pacific sole, scallops, sand dabs, king crab, herring, Pacific flounder, crawfish, Arctic char, and anchovies. If you consume fish of more than two servings in one week, you are advised to take supplements that will aid you in releasing mercury from your body.

WHITE FLOUR

If refined flour is mixed in food, it gets robbed of its natural nutritional content. It is also consisted of lesser vitamins compared to whole grain foods. The parts of the flour that are most nutrient-laden include the germ and the bran but these can't be found in refined flour. The germ and the bran are consisted of such significant vitamins as Zinc, Phosphorus, Magnesium, Thiamin, Folic Acid, and Vitamin E, among others. The bran is also consisted of fiber which is ideal for the digestive system.

The typical white flour that people see in the market doesn't have germ and bran, otherwise, its color wouldn't be white. However, another reason why flour is generally white in color is because it gets bleached. During the bleaching process, the chemicals needed include oxide of nitrogen, nitrosyl, chloride, chlorine, and benzoyl peroxide, then all these will be combined with chemical salts. Chemical residues are not removed from the flour and, sadly, these are health hazards.

Unfortunately, since white flour lacks proper nutrients, it is expected to destabilize your energy field, lower your vibration, and prevent you from channeling high-frequency energies. This only means that if you're serious about mastering Reiki, you must avoid eating white flour products and instead eat whole grain ones.

CAFFEINATED DRINKS

People in general think of coffee when asked what caffeinated beverages are. This is correct but there are other beverages that are also categorized as caffeinated ones. This includes yerba mate, guarana, and caffeinated tea, among others. Some of these drinks have caffeine while some have xanthine, which is a drug that has similar chemical content as the caffeine.

Pretty much like the chocolate, consuming caffeinated drinks improves energy levels, memory, and alertness but only temporarily. After a few hours, consuming a caffeinated drink would most likely distort the functionalities of your nervous system. Apparently, this type of drink results in imbalances as it drains the nerve cells of significant chemicals required for sending Reiki energies of high quality.

If you drink caffeinated drinks, you would notice feeling jittery, nervous, and experience heart palpitations. Yes, it can make you feel awake, thus, allowing you to work overtime. You feel as if your energy level has increased but, in reality, the increased energy level you are experiencing actually takes place in a single part of your nervous system only. Unconsciously, you are unaware that the impact of caffeinated drinks on you is that it lowers your vibration level and, therefore, hinders your capability to reach Reiki energies of high frequency.

ALCOHOL

People who drink alcoholic beverages say that they do so to relax. By drinking, they forget how stressful they are. Alcohol decreases their awareness of pain, both emotional and physical, as well as their need to be a responsible person. Alcohol typically allows them to forget about their present stress and problems, and to falsely boost their confidence.

People who drink alcoholic beverages know that alcohol can be detrimental to their liver and their brain. But, of course, in most cases, they tend to neglect this fact for as long as they don't feel any pain. Sadly, alcohol allows negative energies to enter your body, thus, affecting your aura. Alcohol imbalances your nervous system, your endocrine, and your energy field. It decreases your vibration and prevents you from channeling high-quality energies.

HEAVY METALS

If you're not aware of it, you, and any other living things, are exposed to heavy metals. They are in the food you eat and in your surroundings. Heavy metals could come from industrial pollution or from such natural occurrences as volcanic eruptions. Moreover, if you have dental fillings, you might not be aware that they have mercury content, too.

Mercury and lead are neurotoxins for both the young and the adults. They can decline IQ levels due to the damage they cause to the brain cells. They can lower people's emotional responsiveness too and can cause depression. If these happen to you, as a Reiki practitioner, you might fail to achieve a high emotional state and a high spiritual state of consciousness.

Most, if not all, medical clinics perform tests to determine a person's heavy metal contamination. That way, people would know how to address such health issues as they can either undergo either the dimercaptosuccinic acid (DMSA) test or the ethylenediaminetetraacetic (EDTA) acid. Moreover, there are natural supplements that can be taken to treat health issues gradually. These include homeopathic remedies, chlorella, amino acids, and modified citrus pectin, among others.

RECOMMENDED FOOD

If you're serious about improving the way you perform Reiki sessions, it is best that you take care of yourself by means of being careful with the food you eat. There are several types of healthy diet to choose from. One of the recommended ones is the Fish and Vegetable Diet. There is also the Vegan Diet or the Raw Food Diet. These kinds of diet are guaranteed to help you achieve natural balance in your body system and ultimately help you attract, balance, and channel high-quality Reiki energies.

If your goal is to be the best Reiki practitioner, you must remember that you must improve your lifestyle to ultimately achieve your desired outcome. Enhancing your lifestyle means maintaining a healthy diet, going to the gym, attending yoga sessions, and doing good deeds on a daily basis, among many others.

When you exert your effort to improve your diet, don't forget to apply the mental or emotional symbol as it will guide you in achieving your goals. A proper diet will result in mental clarity, vitality, enhanced energy, better sleep. If and when you achieve all these, you will be highly equipped in handling self-healing sessions as well as healing sessions for others. In other words, taking care of yourself can help you assert your higher purpose.

TIPS FOR DIETING AND EXERCISING

Here are some recommendations on how you can included proper diet and exercise in your Reiki practice on a daily basis:

1. Practice the Fish and Vegetable Diet as it is the most recommended diet of all for Reiki students and

practitioners. There is also the Vegan Diet or the Raw Food Diet. These kinds of diet are guaranteed to help you achieve natural balance in your body system and ultimately help you attract, balance, and channel high-quality Reiki energies.

2. Practice drinking lukewarm water on a daily basis. Avoid drinking refrigerated water because it's not ideal for digestion. At the same time, practice what everybody generally knows about drinking water – drink at least eight glasses a day.

3. Of course, you are highly discouraged to eat food with preservatives or those that can be bought in fast food chains. However, in this fast-paced world, it's sometimes unavoidable to do so. But, try your very best to always eat fresh foods and those that are home-cooked. In fact, while cooking, you can write Reiki symbols on your head, visualizing them to be on top of the food you're cooking. Doing so will further improve the meal's life force energy. This means that anybody who will eat such food will be able to absorb the Reiki energy of healing, aside from the fact that he will receive proper nutrition.

4. Before purchasing foods, check out the nutrition label first. Find out what its chemical content is, as well as the presence of additives and colors. Carefully check all the time if what you're about to eat is healthy or not.

5. As soon as you wake up, take a tablespoonful of apple cider vinegar mixed with lukewarm water.

6. Practice pranayama and yoga on a daily basis.

7. Work out on a regular basis, or on a daily basis for approximately twenty minutes. Sweating due to vigorous exercise is always a good thing.

8. Before you start a work out, a meditation practice, a yoga session, or a Reiki practice, make sure that your

last meal was taken at least two hours before the session. You can't perform a session with a full stomach. Remember to just eat right after the session.

9. Minimize your salt and sugar intake. If you can eliminate them from your diet, please do so as they don't have anything good to do to your mind and body.

10. Strictly follow a schedule when it comes to your diet and exercise. Even on weekends, make sure that your scheduled is strictly followed. It is best if you also have a fixed schedule for waking up and sleeping. Also, make sure that you sleep for approximately eight hours per day.

11. Have you ever heard of the quote, "Sitting is the new smoking"? There is definitely a lot of truth to that. You have to be physically active on a daily basis so make sure that you practice regular walks in your neighborhood and, ideally, in the park. It's also a good time to spend alone.

12. Practice laughing and smiling all the time as both are good for your mind and soul.

Chapter 6 Growing Your Relationship with Reiki

In this chapter, you will learn about how you can ultimately enhance your relationship with Reiki. Apparently, just like how you learn any other thing, the only way to learn this is by exploring your relationship with it. Below are the step-by-step instructions on how to go about it. But, first, you are requested to look for a comfortable area to begin a session. Make sure that you are positioned comfortably. Similar to the other sessions we have discussed here, the most ideal position is sitting on a chair or sitting Indian-style on the floor.

YOUR REIKI CONNECTION

1. Start by taking deep and slow breaths. Then, gently close your eyes. As you do deep breathing, observe the way your shoulders and your neck relax. Make sure that you're sitting up straight. Then, observe the way the other parts of your body relax starting from your arms then to your hands and to your fingers. Then, to your upper back, your lower back, your hips, your thighs, your knees, your lower legs, your ankles, your feet, your sole, and down to your toes. Take your time until you feel that you're in a relaxed and peaceful state.

2. By this time, you should feel more balanced emotionally and physically. Otherwise, continue the process of taking deep and slow breaths while observing the way each part of your body relax.

3. Now, visualize yourself as an emerging Reiki healer. Envision how you think you'd look like when you heal yourself. Then, envision how you think you'd look like when you heal others. What kind of thoughts and emotions should you have?

4. Think about your desire to perform Reiki healing. What are your goals? Why do you want to become a Reiki practitioner and a Reiki healer? What do you hope to achieve? Strongly envision all these.

5. Take your time in doing this exercise. Before you end the session, ask yourself if you're satisfied with it. Otherwise, don't stop yet. You'll actually feel if there's a need to stop the session or if there's a need to go on.

6. Once you're ready, gently open your eyes. It's best if you have a journal where you can record your observations and your goals for becoming a Reiki healer. Make sure that your goals are clear so that the results will be clear as well. This shall be the beginning of your journey towards Reiki healing.

REIKI HEALING STRATEGIES TO ENHANCE EMOTIONAL WELL-BEING

Level 2 Reiki healers have an advantage when it comes to enhancing one's emotional well-being. This is so because during their attunement process, they receive additional Reiki symbols that would greatly help them in healing emotionally-caused illnesses. However, there are alternative techniques that Level 1 Reiki healers may apply in order for them to perform emotional healing. These techniques may also be used by Level 2 Reiki healers as a supplement. Below are the step-by-step instructions on how to go about it:

1. Gently close your eyes and then take deep and slow breaths. Begin welcoming Reiki for the healing session.

2. Healing will begin in your head. It will address such health issues as anxiety, cognitive impairment, emotional overwhelm, and stress. Gently raise and hover your hands above your head, at the Crown Chakra, then move them slowly over your forehead. While doing so, focus on the sensation as Reiki flows through your head. Then, move and hover your hands over the back of your head, and then, over the back of

your neck. Continuously hover your hand over your entire head while feeling the Reiki flowing inside your head.

3. Now, move and hover your hand over your forehead once again. Don't remove your focus on the Reiki flowing through your head. Then, press your palms on each side of your head – your left palm should be pressed on the left side of your head while the right palm should be pressed on the right side of your head.

4. The head stores cognitive processing, emotional processing, fear, worry, and mental energy. If you specifically want to heal issues related to these, simply continue to press your palms on the sides of your head for as long as you want. If there are images or sensations that come up as you do this method, just let them be and accept them. At the same time, allow the Reiki to continuously flow through you to heal such issues.

5. Once you feel like you're ready to proceed to the next technique, press one of your palms on your forehead and then the other on the back of your head, just above your nape. The displaced energy caused by mental exhaustion and headaches will be balanced through this position.

6. If you experience tension headaches, emotional confusion, doubt, and worry, you may hover your hands over the space between your eyebrows or where the Third Eye is located. Then, move your hands in a circular motion.

7. If you experience allergies, emotional fatigue, blurred vision, and eye strain, gently press your palms on your closed eyes. Observe how pressure behind, and at the sides, of your eyes is relieved. Do this also to relieve emotional tension especially if you don't know how to release the negative feelings inside you.

8. If there are stressful or emotional information that you want to stop thinking about, gently press your palms on your ears. This way, Reiki will not allow you to hear unnecessary noise and will prevent you from thinking about negative things. Reiki will enable you to hear and feel positive things only.

9. If you haven't noticed, you tend to grind your teeth or clench your jaws when you feel stressed. This is a common occurrence among stressed people but most people don't notice it because, oftentimes, it happens unconsciously. To allow the Reiki energy to continuously flow through you, gently press the palms of your hands on your jaws while your fingertips rest under each ear. Without removing the palms of your hands on your jaws, allow your fingertips to gently move to and press your temples, then move them back under your ears, touching your earlobes. Do this several times and notice how this activity amazingly makes you feel better.

10. Once you're ready to end your session, create a mental image of a healing and protective shield surrounding your neck and your head. Then, affirm that from now on, you'll be more balanced in terms of releasing and feeling your emotions.

11. Now, gently position your hands side by side, palms facing upward as if asking for alms, as they hover under your chin. As you do this, you will feel the warmth of your breath as you take slow and deep breaths. Continuously do this until you feel peaceful and calm.

12. You may close your Reiki connection once you are satisfied with the session.

This is an ideal technique to practice on a daily basis, specifically right before you start working or right before you start an activity that you know might bring a lot of stress.

You're suggested to apply these techniques on a daily basis and as often as you want to address issues of mental and emotional imbalances. That way, those imbalances will be relieved or will disappear.

Once you have mastered these techniques, you will find yourself somehow modifying some hand techniques. This is alright as long as you feel comfortable doing so and as long as you find it more effective.

TECHNIQUES TO SCAN YOUR AURA

In this section, you will be taught techniques on how to scan your aura or your energetic field. This is important as your aura is an extension of the internal energies of your human body. Aside from your own body, your aura is also influenced by environmental factors such as objects, events, places, and people, among others. If and when you apply the techniques discussed here, you'll become more aware of how both your body and the environment are connected to the state of your aura.

1. Gently close your eyes and start breathing slowly and deeply. Observe how your neck relaxes, as well as your shoulders, arms, elbows, hands, lower back, legs, angles, feet, and toes. Continuously do this until you achieve your most relaxed and comfortable state.

2. Into your hands, invoke Reiki through a method you prefer to apply. The important thing is that you'd be able to effectively feel the healing light of Reiki into the palms of your hands. Then, slowly raise your hands forward and pretend that you're holding an imaginary ball on each hand. Pretend the balls to be the Reiki. Imagine them to look similarly as bright and shiny crystal balls. Gently open your eyes, bring your hands to your lap, and then, hover them above your head and

your body. Repeatedly do this as if the Reiki balls in your hands are scanning your mind and body.

3. The sensation that you feel while your hands hover above your head and body is your energetic field or your aura. You may feel some vibrations or you may visualize colors as your hands hover. You may feel some warm or cold sensation. You will feel different kinds of sensations. You'll notice that the sensations seem to shift from time to time. This is because of the different emotions residing inside you such as anger, anxiety, sadness, and joy.

4. Now, start exploring the energy around you. Raise your arms forward once again and continue to pretend that you're holding an imaginary ball on each of your hand. Stretch your arms as far as you can. Position your palms outward as if you're pushing the ball you're holding as far as you can. Imagine the balls boomeranging around you and eventually returning to your palms. Observe how stronger the positive energies come back to you. As you do this repeatedly, you'll observe that you feel safer and safer.

By doing such technique, Reiki connects you with the energies around you so that you'll have the power to harmonize them.

There's another technique you may use wherein you may hover the imaginary balls on objects or areas that you think need to be connected to positive energies. These could be chairs, doorways, desks, and walls, among many others. You may use the same technique if you're outdoors. You may hover your palms on plants, the wind, the water, and even on earth. Observe how it feels as you do this technique.

It is best if you could document your experiences in your journal. That way, you get to review your observations and compare your new and old experiences. Notice how much you've improved in applying this technique.

Once you're done, you may clasp your hands together to signalize that you're ending your connection to Reiki. Don't forget to thank Reiki for guidance.

REIKI FOR OLD PEOPLE, YOUNG PEOPLE, AND EVEN ANIMALS

As previously mentioned, Reiki healing may be applied to all living things not just to heal a disease, but also to address emotional issues, spiritual issues, and others. Reiki is for everyone. It can be applied to children, the middle-aged, and the aged. It can, of course, also be applied to animals, regardless of its age.

When conducting Reiki healing on animals or babies, the hand techniques to be applied are basically the same. Unlike adults who are mindful of their actions, expect both animals and babies – and even elderly people – to move a lot during the session. This means that you have to be creative when healing them. It doesn't matter if you can't seem to apply the exact hand positions during the session. The important thing is that you're healing them effectively. Be mindful of their behavior and observe what they're trying to communicate to you. They can't speak that's why you have to be observant of their actions and reactions. At first, you'll find this to be a challenging session but, eventually, you'll realize that it's fun after all.

There are times though when conducting such session can also be challenging. In cases like this, you may apply the distant healing methods instead. This is effective even if you're in the same room.

There are ideal instances when the children, elderly, and animals can best receive Reiki healing:

- After being born (for children and animals);

- If they have an illness (but seeing a doctor or a veterinarian is still highly recommended);

- If they experience trauma; and

- If they want to maintain a balanced energy; among other instances.

You have the option to send Reiki energy to their medication, their water, and their food too. This will help boost positive Reiki energy.

FAMILIARIZE YOURSELF WITH THE BEHAVIOR OF ANIMALS, BABIES, AND OLD PEOPLE

The old people, babies, and animals are all fragile beings. Expect them to respond differently from people aged between 20 and 60. Here are some guidelines that will help you anticipate their behavior:

- Expect a baby to cry hysterically. Expect a dog to bark or growl nonstop. Expect other animals to hiss, fly, and make other distracting noises especially if they don't want to be touched. Expect all of them to make loud noises because they may be in extreme pain or trauma. If you find it difficult to touch them, you may instead apply the distant healing techniques.

- At first, it might seem as if they're allowing you to touch them. However, there'll be times when they will shift from one position to another any time they want to. This might be a challenge for you to apply the Reiki healing techniques. If they keep on moving and don't seem that they'd want to keep still, you might want to opt to the distant Reiki healing methods.

- You'd know if an animal badly wants to receive Reiki healing. It will come near you. It may create sounds especially if it's in pain but it'll stay near you.

- It the animal seems to shift its behavior from being tame to wild, you may also shift to distant healing instead. That way, you're not at risk.

Chapter 7 Tools Used By Reiki Practitioners

Once you have mastered Reiki healing, you might eventually become interested in putting up your own healing center or healing service. If that's the case, there are several tools that you have to invest in. Below are the tools necessary for your professional Reiki healing practice:

THE REIKI TABLE

The Reiki table is the most important item that you have to purchase. Even if you haven't completed the Level 2 Reiki program but you already want to work with clients, you are advised to invest heavily in this item.

Choose a massage table that has a similar feel to that of a comfortable mattress because Reiki highly promotes comfort and relaxation. You have to ensure its softness and durability and, most importantly, you have to choose a product that's not costly.

There are portable Reiki tables that are convenient to assemble. You might want to look for something like this for easy storage. Besides, its' not all the time that you'll need to use a Reiki table. There are times when your patients would prefer sitting down on the floor or standing up. If this is the case, at least it's easy for you to assemble and disassemble the Reiki table.

There are several factors that you need to consider when buying a Reiki table:

1. THE HEIGHT OF THE REIKI TABLE HAS TO BE ADJUSTABLE. Of course, your patients are not of the same height so, therefore, your Reiki table should be adjustable. At the same time, an adjustable table means that you may lower its height if you prefer to conduct

your healing session while you sit down or you may increase the height if you prefer to stand up. In doing so, it's not only your patient who becomes comfortable but also you. Remember, any kind of discomfort that you feel will be a distraction to your Reiki healing methods.

2. THE REIKI TABLE HAS TO BE PORTABLE. Most Reiki tables available in the market are portable and it's up to you to choose what kind of portable table you'd want to purchase. The important thing to consider is how practical your choice is for you. For instance, you might want to opt for a table with additional springs and knobs because this type of table will allow you to set up faster than the other types of Reiki tables available. You might also opt for a table with built-in handles to make it easier for you to carry it anywhere you want.

3. THE REIKI TABLE HAS TO BE A COMFORTABLE ONE. Of course, when you're conducting a Reiki healing session, you're not the only one who's supposed to feel comfortable. Your patient also has to be in his most comfortable state to ensure that the healing session is effective.

If your patient prefers a lying position, chances are that he'd be lying on the Reiki table for a minimum of 30 minutes. In that case, it's indeed important that he's lying comfortable on the table. This means that when you're at the store looking for the perfect Reiki table to buy, always take into consideration the firmness, durability, softness, and thickness of the product. If you want your patient to come back to you for your services, then you have to give them an ultimate Reiki healing experience – and letting them lie down on a comfortable and relaxing table is one way of doing so. Make them feel that visiting your healing center is not the same as visiting a doctor's office.

4. THE REIKI TABLE SHOULD BE ABLE TO SUPPORT HEAVY WEIGHT PATIENTS. You must ensure that your Reiki table can support even those who are heavy weight. The table must not make any creaking noise when your patient moves. It should not shake or snap. When looking for a Reiki table to purchase, check the materials used to make the product. Check its durability and overall quality to ensure the safety of your patients.

THE FACE CRADLE

The face cradle is also an important item to invest in. A comfortable Reiki table definitely matches a comfortable face cradle to allow the patient to achieve an ultimate Reiki experience. Of course, during the Reiki healing session, you will not instruct your patient to lie down on his back all the time. There are times when your patient has to lie on his stomach in which, of course, he also has to be in a comfortable state.

A Reiki table is manufactured with a universal design and, therefore, any type of face cradle that you see in the market will easily attach and fit to the table that you will buy. This is a good thing because you don't have to take into consideration how well it will fit to the table. You can instead focus on the softness, durability, and comfort of the face cradle.

THE REIKI TABLE SHEETS

Make your patient as comfortable as possible by also covering your Reiki table with clean and comfortable sheets. There are several factors that you may consider when looking for the most ideal Reiki table sheets:

1. THE REIKI TABLE SHEETS HAVE TO HAVE BREATHABLE FABRIC. Covering your Reiki table with such type of fabric will prevent your patient from getting itchy, overheated, and uncomfortable while lying down. Remember that before you begin the Reiki

healing session, your patient has to be in his most comfortable state. Besides, seeing your patient lying in the table in his most comfortable state will definitely make you feel comfortable as well.

2. THE REIKI TABLE SHEETS HAVE TO BE OIL-RESISTANT. There are Reiki healers who apply massage grade oils or essential oils when they conduct Reiki healing sessions. If you're a beginner, you might not yet consider using these oils. However, as you progress, you will eventually try to use them. Maybe, you will not use them on a regular basis but there will definitely come a time when you will use these oils from time to time. Therefore, it is best that you choose a Reiki table sheet fabric that is oil-resistant. Otherwise, your fabric might be permanently ruined.

3. THE REIKI TABLE SHEETS HAVE TO BE HYPOALLERGENIC. Always take into consideration the fact that your patients will all be different from one another. There will be patients who won't have any complaints at all while there will be patients who have sensitive skin and might not agree to lie down in your Reiki table if your sheets are not hypoallergenic.

This factor is significant as a sheet that's not hypoallergenic might eventually transfer sweat, dead skin, hair, bacteria, and dust mites to another patient. This type of Reiki table sheet is expected to be more expensive than the other types of sheets. Nonetheless, it's effective, it provides comfort, and it provides safety to your patients. It's also durable which makes it a good investment to make.

Chapter 8 Techniques for Detecting and Healing Negative Energies

In this chapter, you will specifically learn how to detect and heal negative energies. It is important that you know how to identify negative energies and heal them immediately. That way, you will be able to address energetic blockage issues residing inside your patients. But, of course, before you detect and heal you patients' negative energies, you should be able to address your own energetic blockage issues first.

BEGIN

To start, take deep and slow breaths and then gently close your eyes. Reflect on your current emotional state and be mindful of how you feel. If you feel negative emotions, simply accept and acknowledge that feeling. Be mindful of which parts of your body feel pain, pressure, and numbness because these are where the energetic blockages are residing.

INTUITION

Use your intuition to visualize how the blockages look like. Take your time to process the sensations that you feel and the memories that come up. As soon as these emotions and memories become vivid, it means that you're prepared to heal yourself.

BREATH

As you continue to repeatedly take slow and deep breaths, allow Reiki to enter through your hands. Then, hover your hands to where you feel the energetic blockages are residing. As you hover your hands, envision those blockages disappearing through the help of Reiki. You'll notice that more and more negative memories are resurfacing. Simply acknowledge those memories.

FOCUS

It is possible that your hands will stop feeling warm. If this happens, it means that your energetic blockages are deep. Simply ask Reiki to guide you in dissolving the blockages. Keep in mind that Reiki and the positive energies are more powerful than those negative energies. Strongly focus on the fact that all blockages will soon be dissolved.

FEEL

There are times when the energetic blockages are not dissolved during the first session. Some blockages are dissolved after conducting several sessions. Don't give up if this happens. The important thing is that after every session, you feel better and better.

THANKS

Once you feel prepared to end the session, gently clasp your hands together. After every session, don't forget to thank Reiki for the guidance. Thank Reiki for alleviating the blockages. Then, affirm that soon, all blockages will eventually be removed.

JOURNAL

Again, it is advisable that you document your experiences in your journal. Write about your mental images, the sounds you hear, the colors you see, the shapes that you see, and the sensations that you feel. If you keep on doing this over and over again, you'll observe how big – or small – your progress has become. In time, you'll eventually learn how to conveniently address such negative emotions.

Conclusion

I'd like to thank you and congratulate you for transiting my lines from start to finish.

I hope this book was able to help you understand everything that you basically need to know about Reiki. The topics are all explained in such a way that can be understood as easily as possible because that's basically what Reiki wants to convey – that life should be lived without complication and that life should be lived in a positive manner.

This book is ideal for the following:

- Anyone interested in becoming a Reiki Master;
- Anyone interested in knowing more about Reiki;
- Anyone who wants to have a positive outlook in life;
- Anyone who wants emotional, physical, and mental healing;
- Anyone who wants to help others heal emotionally, physically, and mentally; and
- Reiki practitioners who want to enhance their knowledge of Reiki; among many others.

The next step is to find the ideal Reiki Master for you. Choose a Reiki Master whom you think will become your mentor. Every Reiki Master has his own expertise. For sure, every Reiki Master is an ideal mentor. But there will always be a specific person that you'd feel the most comfortable with. Nobody else can choose this but you.

I wish you the best of luck!

Thanks for Reading!

What did you think of, **Autoimmune Healing Transform Your Health, Reduce Inflammation, Heal The Immune System and Start Living Healthy**

I know you could have picked any number of books to read, but you picked this book and for that I am extremely grateful.

I hope that it added at value and quality to your everyday life. If so, it would be really nice if you could share this book with your friends and family by posting to Facebook and Twitter.

If you enjoyed this book and found some benefit in reading this, I'd like to hear from you and hope that you could take some time to post a review. Your feedback and support will help this author to greatly improve his writing craft for future projects and make this book even better.

I want you, the reader, to know that your review is very important and so, if you'd like to leave a review, all you have to do is click here and away you go. I wish you all the best in your future success!

Also check out my other book:

Autoimmune Healing Transform Your Health, Reduce Inflammation, Heal The Immune System and Start Living Healthy

Thank you and good luck!

Madison Fuller 2019

Claim your FREE Audiobook Now

Autoimmune Healing: Transform Your Health, Reduce Inflammation, Heal the Immune System and Start Living Healthy

Do you have an overall sense of not feeling your best, but it has been going on so long that it's actually normal to you?

If you answered yes to any of these question, you may have an autoimmune disease.

Autoimmune diseases are one of the ten leading causes of death for women in all age groups and they affect nearly 25 million Americans. In fact millions of people worldwide suffer from autoimmunity whether they know it or not.

The good news is that many autoimmune conditions can be reversed through a targeted protocol designed to heal the autoimmune system.

AUTOIMMUNE HEALING

Transform Your Health, Reduce Inflammation,
Heal The Immune System and Start Living Healthy

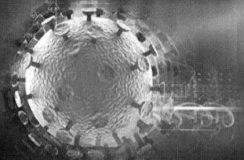

MADISON FULLER

A SPIRITUAL START!

Start your week with gratitude, joy, inspiration, and love.
Healing, motivation, inspiration, challenge and guidance straight to your inbox every week!

FIND OUT MORE

Printed in Great Britain
by Amazon

47790296R00071